God's Land on Loan

God's Land on Loan
Israel, Palestine, and the World

W. Eugene March

Westminster John Knox Press
LOUISVILLE • LONDON

© 2007 W. Eugene March

Previously published as *Israel and the Politics of Land: A Theological Case Study* (Louisville, KY: Westminster/John Knox Press, 1994).

Book design by Drew Stevens
Cover design by Eric Walljasper, Minneapolis, MN

First edition
Published by Westminster John Knox Press
Louisville, Kentucky

This book is printed on acid-free paper that meets the American National Standards Institute Z39.48 standard. ∞

PRINTED IN THE UNITED STATES OF AMERICA

07 08 09 10 11 12 13 14 15 16 — 10 9 8 7 6 5 4 3 2 1

Library of Congress Cataloging-in-Publication Data

March, W. Eugene (Wallace Eugene).
  God's land on loan : Israel, Palestine, and the world / W. Eugene March.
    p. cm.
  Includes bibliographical references and index.
  ISBN 978-0-664-23151-4 (alk. paper)
  1. Land tenure—Religious aspects—Christianity. 2. Land tenure—Israel. 3. Land tenure—Palestine. 4. Environmental protection—Israel.
5. Environmental protection—Palestine. 6. Stewardship, Christian. I. Title.
  BR115.L23M23   2007
  231.7'6—dc22   20067007765

Contents

Preface

This book is primarily about land and how we think about it. It is written from a Christian perspective, which means at the least that the Bible is an important underpinning and that the transformation of human society is an acknowledged goal. Reformation and reconciliation are important to Christians. Justice is a standard we hold especially high. Compassion is the mode of justice.

The thesis of this book is that land is best understood as a divine loan intended for responsible (righteous and just) use. Human communities require land, but they can never claim full ownership and are ever to be judged by how they exercise dominion over the land. The biblical account concerning ancient Israel is the primary basis for this thesis. The Bible presents standards by which to measure conflicting claims about and uses of land in this one world we all inhabit.

As a means of sharpening theological insight about land, I concentrate here upon a specific piece of land that has been of interest to many people for many centuries. This land is located at the eastern end of the Mediterranean Sea and serves as a bridge between Africa and Asia. The earliest biblical sources call this bridge the "land of Canaan." The Romans named it "Palestine." For more than four thousand years, armies have marched back and forth through this area as various nations have sought domination. A better understanding of the history and significance of this land and its people is an additional goal of this study.

The land in question is now known as Israel. Israel is a small country; more than half of its population is concentrated in the coastal plain, a narrow band of arable land about 170 miles long from north to south and about 10 to 25 miles wide. The interior of the land is hilly and rocky. On the eastern side of the land is the Jordan Valley, and to the south is the Negev Desert. From the extreme northern point to the southernmost point is 260 miles, and from east to west the distance at the widest is 72 miles. If the territory that Israel has occupied since 1967 is included, the country is about the size of Maryland.

The attention that Israel receives far exceeds its size, resources, or strategic location (which is not nearly as significant in our modern world as it was in antiquity). The creation of modern Israel on land once occupied by the biblical Israelites is one major reason for the scrutiny. Some see this as the fulfillment of ancient prophecy. Others see it as part of an imperialist plot. Still others see Israel as a haven for Jews in a world where the hatred of Jews is still rampant. Jews, Christians, and Muslims all claim a special relationship with the place, a fact that heightens sensitivities all the more.

The level of interest that Israel and the Middle East command was made dramatically clear in the summer of 2006 when Israel, in retaliation for continuing harassment from Palestinians, launched a devastating attack on Lebanon. Peace negotiations that had languished seem now to be totally derailed. But many Israelis and Palestinians long for peace and remain willing to work toward it. There have been many setbacks since the first serious efforts were made in the early 1990s, but there is still the possibility that actual peace involving the construction of two independent geopolitical states might emerge. Israel and the Palestinians, along with some of the neighboring Arab states, have made sputtering moves toward defining a new relationship. Central to that relationship is the mutual recognition of the several parties and a commitment to work toward a resolution of the vast differences that have separated Israel and the Palestinians. The recognition of Israel's right to exist and a guarantee of secure borders have, at long last, been acknowledged by some of the parties involved. Equally important, the need to enable the Palestinians to establish a viable national entity with an adequate economy and self-rule is also widely acknowledged. The ultimate resolution of the many land issues yet lies in the future, but all the parties may finally be at the right place to make the effort possible.

While one of my goals is to enable readers, especially North American Christians, to become better informed about the history and significance of modern Israel, I also have a wider objective, namely to further an understanding and appreciation of God's claim on all land. The search for a just peace in the Middle East involves knowledge about the peculiar history of the peoples of the area. But the principles that guide the search can be applied to any conflict over land—whether in the Middle East, Central America, the United States, or wherever.

Central to any effort to work toward reformation and reconciliation is the conviction that God alone is Creator and Adjudicator. God has created the world and appointed human beings as "earth keepers." We are all held accountable in accordance with this divine appointment. It is hoped that reflection about a particular place, modern Israel, may help us to understand more concretely the possibilities, both positive and negative, of exercising dominion over any land. The wider goal is to recognize and work toward faithfully fulfilling our God-given roles as earth keepers wherever we live.

This book is intended as a contribution toward understanding the significance of land, God's land, and to its just and righteous use. If I have incorrectly interpreted the views of others, they are honest mistakes, not malicious distortions. It is certainly my hope that any misunderstandings can be corrected and that they will not stand in the way of the wider views of this book. As earth keepers we are obligated to right injustices and to secure peace wherever possible. Such a mandate requires that we get on with the task.

A special word of thanks is due to Rabbi Vernon Kurtz (North Suburban Synagogue Beth El, Highland Park, IL) for his careful reading of and valuable suggestions for this revised volume. Numerous persons from Highland Presbyterian Church and from The Temple in Louisville, Kentucky, contributed their critical and helpful insights to the first version of this work. The staff at Westminster John Knox Press, especially Jack Keller, have provided much-appreciated encouragement and support. To one and all, thank you.

1

People and the Land

Many Faces, Many Voices

This book is about land and some theological insights about the way humans are connected with land. It begins by focusing on a very special land, Israel/Palestine, which has claimed the attention of many, many people across the past three millennia or more. Especially have the adherents of three of the world's great religions—Judaism, Christianity, and Islam—shown continuing interest in this land, which they have often called the "promised land" or the "holy land," with Jerusalem being the "holy city" or in Arabic, *al-Quds*. What is more, this relatively small piece of geography, about the size of the state of Maryland, has, for centuries, been at the center of military strategy and political intrigue. This territory, controlled largely by the government of modern Israel at the present, has received and continues to receive more attention per square mile than perhaps any other area in the world.

To begin to understand something of the attraction of this land, we will start with the people who live on the land. This beginning point is chosen for several reasons. First, the people of Israel are fascinating in their multiplicity and diversity. Many who have never visited Israel are amazed by the wide variety of people who live within this small country. Israel is in some ways a microcosm of our world, with many ethnic, language, racial, and religious communities. People from all over the world have immigrated to Israel to join with many whose families have always lived in Palestine/Israel—some Jews, some Christians, and some Muslims. The reality of the diversity of Israel's population quickly challenges and shatters the stereotypes that many have of this land. This is not a homogeneous society by any standard of measure.

Second, the people in Israel tend to hold strong views about their land. Often, they have a greater attachment to particular parcels of land than is usually expressed by urbanites in Europe or the United States. Many people in Israel, Muslims and Jews alike, are prepared to fight and even die for their land, identifying themselves with the land in a way that seems to go beyond mere nationalism. To begin to understand these people is to gain insight into how questions about the land might be framed and addressed. To ignore the people living on the land so central to the biblical accounts would surely be a mistake.

Third, the people who live on the land express a number of contrasting views about the significance and importance of land. For some their land is a divine legacy never to be compromised. For others their land is a place to live and raise their families as they see fit in light of their own worldviews. For still others land is a bargaining chip in the ongoing struggle for a secure peace. If anyone were tempted to believe there is a single Jewish position or a single Arab understanding or a single Christian teaching about land in general or about the land of Israel/Palestine in particular, speaking with people who live in modern Israel will at least give serious cause for hesitancy. Before fashioning any broad, general view about the theological significance of land, it is important to listen to and reflect upon what real people have to say about their particular land. This is a crucial topic, and Israel's pluralism regarding this matter is critical to recognize and hear.

Finally, to begin this book with the views of the people who inhabit Israel/Palestine requires an acknowledgment of the centuries-long struggles provoked by claims about and over land. To talk about land in the abstract would surely be a disservice. Land takes on significance because it is claimed, fought for, tilled, built upon, treasured, and loved by human beings. The passions and controversies encountered in Israel are reflections of similar feelings and commitments held by other human communities around the globe. Any wider theological reflection about land should be informed by the reality of the conflicts, the injustices, and the vision that land evokes in any particular space. Some believe that the only solution is to quit talking about land altogether and stress the oneness and unity of humankind. The reality of Israel/Palestine, however, argues not for less reflection and talk about land, but for more. Thus, the people of Israel/Palestine—for whom the debate over land is vigorous—offer an appropriate beginning place for the discussion.

THE SETTING

The nation Israel is a parliamentary democracy, and its multi-party political system reflects the cultural, ethnic, and ideological diversity of Israel's population. The openness and freedom of its debates are uncommon in most of the Middle East. A multiplicity of opinions about almost every significant issue is readily apparent in Israel and is considered a national value.

By history and tradition, Jerusalem is the preeminent city in Israel. Its population of approximately 718,000 reflects the cultural, ethnic, religious, and political diversity of the country more clearly than any other city or region. Israel declared the whole of Jerusalem its capital in 1980, an action still disputed by many governments around the world. At the center of this modern city is a very old section known as the Old City. Surrounded by a wall about two and a half miles long built in 1537 CE by the Ottoman ruler Sultan Suleiman the Magnificent, the Old City peculiarly exemplifies the cultural and religious diversity of contemporary Israel. For many centuries, Muslims, Christians, and Jews have occupied parts of this town.

Sometimes one group banned others, but each group was always aware of the others and the claims of tradition that each group had on this place.

Some of the most ancient remains of biblical Jerusalem have been uncovered within the Old City, and some of the most modern tensions are being lived out here. The people who go in and out of the Old City are a microcosm of Israeli society. Spending time at two historic gates into the Old City, Damascus Gate and Jaffa Gate, provides a dramatic illustration of the diversity of Israel's population and the multiplicity of views about land.

THE PEOPLE OF DAMASCUS GATE

Damascus Gate is the most elaborate of the eight gates into the Old City. This creation of Suleiman rests upon the remains of a gate dated to the second century CE. The gate is situated on the north side of the Old City and is the most direct means of access to the Muslim and Christian sectors. The name of the gate in itself is a testimony to the diversity of those who use it and the controversy among them. Arabs call it *Bab el Amud* (Pillar Gate) for a pillar associated with the gate from which the distance to Damascus, the destination of the original road, was measured, a little over 150 miles. Jews, particularly in recent years, call the gate *Shaar Shekhem* (Shechem Gate) because the road leads north to the site of biblical Shechem (now surrounded by the modern Arab city Nablus), around 30 miles to the north.

An hour at Damascus Gate provides enormous insight into Israel's diversity. It is difficult to describe the various sounds and smells on a busy morning. At the top and slightly to the west of the sloping entrance to the gate is one of the main thoroughfares and shopping streets of East Jerusalem. A major Israeli military checkpoint monitors traffic and provides a visible reminder of who is in control of Jerusalem these days. People—all manner of people—come and go. Around the entrance to the gate, vendors sell their wares. Voices rise and fall as people haggle over prices. Much of it is common tourist stuff, but many different types of food add to the aroma of the place as well. There are animals—donkeys and, especially, cats; camels are seen less frequently in recent years. A delivery boy runs pell-mell down the sloping incline to the gate, his cart bouncing every few feet on a step while the load sways from side to side. Men, women, and children move in and out of the gate offering a panorama of the some two hundred thousand Arabs residing in and around the Old City.

Approximately 1.4 million Arabs, or some 20 percent of Israel's total population of roughly 7.1 million residents, are citizens of Israel. Approximately another 2 million Arabs live under Israeli control but are not citizens. Most of Israel's Arabs are Sunni Muslims, the larger of the two major sects of Islam and by far the largest group within Israel and Palestine. Arabs of the other group are known as Shiites and live mainly in Iraq and Iran. The division occurred shortly after the death of the Prophet Muhammad and originally centered on whether rulers (caliphs) could be descendants only of Ali, Muhammad's son-in-law (the Shiite position), or could be elected from Muhammad's tribe (the Sunni position). Today the Shiites consider themselves to be the more conservative and enthusiastic proponents of Islam.

Within the largely Muslim Arab population is an important subgroup, namely the Christians. They are Eastern Orthodox, Oriental Orthodox (Armenian Orthodox, Coptic Orthodox, Ethiopian Orthodox, and Syrian Orthodox); Catholics (Armenian, Latin-rite, Marionite, Melkite, Syrian); Anglicans and members of several Protestant denominations (Assemblies of God, Baptist, Church of the Nazarene, Episcopal, Lutheran, Methodist, Presbyterian, and others). While not all the Christians in Israel are Arabs, approximately 9 percent are. Some Arab Christians trace their ancestry to pre-Islamic days in Palestine. Nazareth in the Galilee, for instance, the place of Jesus' childhood, and a town of over seventy thousand, was once largely Christian, with many inhabitants who traced their roots back to the earliest centuries of the Common Era. Today the population is 55–60 percent Muslim. Further, about forty thousand Israeli Jews occupy what is known as Upper Nazareth. Many Christians who lived in the area have left the country. Nonetheless, in a number of municipalities in the Galilee, Christian Arabs continue to occupy key positions, being particularly prominent in education and service agencies.

For the most part, the people streaming through the Damascus Gate are not wealthy. Their clothes are not stylish and are patched and well worn. Shopping bags contain mainly necessities. Their eyes show the weariness and the wariness common to people for whom life is an unrelenting struggle. Some older Arab men wear full-length robes as outer garments as well as the traditional headdress, a *keffiyeh*. Most men, however, wear Western-style suits, with and without a *keffiyeh*. While younger women and girls wear skirts and blouses, most of the older women wear long, loose-fitting, cloaklike gowns. Few Arab women in Israel wear veils. Among the throng one may see a Greek Orthodox priest in a long robe or Roman Catholic nuns in traditional garments. Those walking in and out include business and professional people going about their duties, shoppers, and school children.

ARAB VOICES AND VIEWS

Were we to stop some of those hurrying by and ask why they are in this place and in this land, we would get a variety of responses. Pressing them to explain why they are here can be interesting. The answers reflect values that are sometimes not so obvious. Each of the following examples is a fictional person drawn from interviews with many Arabs and Jews in Jerusalem.

Muyad lives in the Dheisheh refugee camp near Bethlehem. A Muslim, he was not even born when his grandparents fled from

Jaffa (Joppa in the Bible) during the 1948 war. He and his family have lived in the camp for more than fifty years, which deeply colors his perspective. Now twenty and a third-generation refugee, Muyad works as a day laborer, whenever he can get work. That is why he is in Jerusalem now. He longs to return to Jaffa. His family has described the family home, the neighborhood, the schools, the market. He has been given the keys to the familial home, though that house has long been gone. In fact the whole area has changed and Jaffa is now a part of Tel Aviv. New streets, plazas, shops, and apartments stand in the place of the old neighborhoods. To Muyad, though, it still exists, at least in his imagination, and one day he hopes, expects, intends to return and claim what is his. He is at the Damascus Gate only because he cannot go home, home to Jaffa. But one day, he believes, he will. His birthright is a small parcel of land overlooking the Mediterranean Sea, and he intends to claim it. What's more, he will not be content until the whole of Palestine—the entire mandate ruled by Great Britain before 1948—is once again in Arab hands.

Miriam, a middle-aged Christian Arab, offers a similar account. Her village was destroyed decades ago. She is a teacher and has found her way to Jerusalem, where she lives with relatives. She has a deep commitment to assist her Palestinian neighbors, both Muslim and Christian. Unlike many of her friends who want to leave Palestine and go to the United States, Miriam feels a sense of vocation to Palestinian children. This place, this land, is theirs by right of habitation and biblical mandate. She vehemently denies Jewish claims to the land. She considers herself one of the rightful offspring of Abraham and Sarah. Her people were in Palestine long before it became modern Israel, and thus her sense of vocation is complemented by a deep sense of belonging to this place. She has no dream of reclaiming and rebuilding her village in the Galilee, but she cannot imagine leaving her homeland. Her attitude toward Israel is resigned hostility.

For Paul, a seventy-year-old Armenian Christian who has lived in Jerusalem his entire life, his passion for this place centers on the holy sites. He has watched as over the years more and more Christians have left. Political and economic hardships have driven many out, and the pressures have increased dramatically over the past decade. Paul grieves that those in the West do not seem to care about maintaining a Christian presence in Jerusalem. His forebears came as early as the fifth century CE, but now the Christian population of Jerusalem, and of Israel as a whole, is declining dramatically. Who will care for the ancient shrines? Who will maintain the ancient rites? If Christ is forgotten here, of all places, what hope can there be? Paul worries about these matters.

Faida, a young Arab woman of twenty, is from a small village south of Nablus. Her whole life has been lived under the Israeli occupation that began with the 1967 war. She and her family are Muslims and have struggled under the military administration. One of her brothers was arrested in a general roundup of Arab youths several months ago and is being detained by the authorities without specific charges. Faida has attended the university in Ramallah, which at the moment is closed by military order. She would not ordinarily be in Jerusalem but came in to visit relatives. She is intensely aware of the limitations that the Israeli occupation has placed on her generation. She wants Israeli forces to withdraw and allow her people to govern themselves. She dreams not about a return of land lost, but about a release of land held captive. Faida's family was not driven out nor have they fled, but they live under military occupation and long for independence. They have land but are not free. Faida's dream is for her own nation, a Palestinian state, alongside Israel if need be, where Palestinians can have their own way of life, their own institutions, their independence. Israel has a right to exist, but it should allow Palestinians that same right and leave the occupied territories.

Ali, a handsome young Muslim of eighteen, is hesitant to talk with strangers. His identity papers are not in order. He is not employed and sees little likelihood of ever being able to support himself or have a family of his own. His hatred for the "occupiers" is deep. He admires the courage and dedication of the young men and women who have volunteered to become suicide bombers. He is not certain whether to make the same decision or not, but he wants to find some way to demonstrate his conviction that the Jews, indeed Westerners in general, have no right to Palestine and should be forced out of the land. One day, he hopes, because of the resistance and martyrdom of young people like himself, the some 770,000 Arabs, in his view forced by the Jews to leave Palestine, will be able to return and once again claim their ancestral land, their heritage. He intends to find a way to enable such a happening, but he has no expectation of personally enjoying the benefits of such a glorious victory.

We could hear other Arab voices if we stayed long enough at Damascus Gate. An Israeli Arab would reflect on the difficulties posed by the dual identity of being Arab and a citizen of Israel. The 1.4 million Israeli Arabs often feel they are second-class citizens in terms of educational and career opportunities. They do not serve in Israel's armed forces. Nonetheless, they are protected under Israeli law, have a passport, vote in Israel's elections, and can be elected to public office. They are constantly torn between conflicting allegiances to the cause of the non-Israeli Arabs, on the one hand, and their own self-interest, on the other. Yes, we could hear other voices, but we must go to another gate, to Jaffa Gate, to listen to others, to Jews who make up approximately 80 percent of Israel's population.

THE PEOPLE OF JAFFA GATE

Jaffa Gate (*Shaar Yafo*, in Hebrew) is located on the western side of the Old City. The road leading to Jaffa on the coast, approximately thirty-five miles away, begins here. This gate is much less elaborate architecturally than Damascus Gate. What's more, the old gate has been widened to allow small trucks and other vehicular traffic to enter. While another gate, Dung Gate on the south, gives easiest access to the Western Wall (formerly known as the "Wailing Wall"), the major Jewish religious site in the Old City, Jaffa Gate for nontourists is probably the most important entry point into the Jewish section of the Old City. It is not that Arabs cannot use this gate, which they call *Bab el Khalil* ("the gate of the friend" in reference to the city of Hebron that takes its name from Abraham, the friend of God; Isa. 41:8), nor that Jews cannot enter at the Damascus Gate; members of each group can and do use them both. Local custom, however, keeps more Jews using Jaffa Gate and more Arabs at Damascus Gate.

The very existence of these two gates is a vivid symbol of the deep division between Jews and Arabs in Israel. Many Jews have little or no contact with Arabs. Even in Jerusalem, which still has a significant concentration of Arabs, it is possible for Jews and Arabs to avoid serious contact almost completely. Arabs fill the menial-service and construction positions, but Jews can ignore them easily enough. To be sure, Jaffa Gate is nearer the new part of Jerusalem where most Jews live, while Damascus Gate is opposite the older part of the city, mainly Arab East Jerusalem. But the symbolism of these two gates is more significant than their actual usage.

Jaffa Gate does not have the same hubbub as Damascus Gate; things at Jaffa Gate are more orderly. Sights, sounds, and smells caress the senses more than they assault them. The people going in and out are better dressed, and more family groups are seen walking together. Jaffa Gate provides ready access to Jewish shops that by and large sell a higher quality of merchandise. There are art galleries and archaeological excavations to visit, and nearby are several religious schools. All of these factors affect the number and kinds of people using Jaffa Gate. Time spent here offers insights that are as valuable as those gained at the Damascus Gate.

JEWISH VOICES AND VIEWS

Rachel, for instance, is nineteen years old, a *sabra* (a native-born Israeli), in the second year of her mandatory military service. In her fatigues, with her weapon slung over her shoulder, she epitomizes a major segment of Israeli society. She has grown up in a world where constant military preparedness has been a necessity. She is determined that no one will destroy her nation, and the pride and confidence in her dark, flashing eyes are unmistakable. She would rather find a peaceful way to live with Arab neighbors and is ready for her government to negotiate peace for land so long as the borders are appropriate and secure. But when use of force is necessary, she believes doing so is fully justified. Like a majority of the Jews in Israel, she is not religious. For her, "Jewishness" is a matter of identity, not primarily a question of religious observance. She is Jewish, and her nation is Jewish. All Jews, secular and religious, have a place in Israel. Others are welcome so long as they acknowledge the right of Israel to exist as a Jewish state. Rachel believes she has a right to this land because she is here. She is Israeli! There is no other place she wants to live.

Bernie is the forty-five-year-old son of parents who fled Nazi Germany in 1940. Many of his distant relatives died in the Holocaust. Life has not been easy for Bernie. His family was destitute when they arrived in Palestine. Eventually, after the 1948 War of Independence, Bernie's father opened a small grocery store. A few years after Bernie's birth, his father died. All his life, Bernie has struggled to get by. Now that his mother is dead and his oldest brother was killed during the Yom Kippur war in 1973, Bernie longs to go to the United States. He has a sense of loyalty to Israel and certainly hopes it will have a secure and fruitful future. But he wants out—out of military service, out of an economic situation marked by high inflation and limited opportunity, out of personal frustration. Bernie has no religious convictions that make it necessary for him to live in Israel. He could be as Jewish as he wants to be in the United States and would certainly have more opportunity to better himself financially. He keeps working and frankly hopes to meet an American woman who will marry him and provide him a way out of Israel. Bernie cares for his nation, but his personal situation is more compelling, and the United States looks like the answer.*

David, age thirty-eight, is an American-born engineer who moved to Jerusalem ten years ago. He grew up on Long Island, went to school in Baltimore, and then worked there. He is a thoughtful, deeply religious man. After a trip to Israel to visit relatives and see the country, David decided to move to Jerusalem to participate in the miracle of Israel. Although he still retains his U.S. citizenship, he is certain that God is responsible for Israel's rebirth as a nation out of the horrors of the Holocaust and for the preservation of this small country despite the surrounding hostile powers. For David, Israel's right to exist is God given; the deed to the land is in the Bible. He is enthusiastic about reclaiming biblical place names, like Shechem for Nablus, Samaria and Judea for the West Bank. The appropriate boundaries of Israel are those of the kingdom of David and Solomon, the land promised to Abraham by God. Israel is God's special nation, and David is certain it will prevail.

Holding somewhat similar views, but coming from quite a different background, is Dvorah, age twenty-eight. She lives with her husband and three children in a settlement about fifteen miles north of Jerusalem and comes to the city only rarely. Like David, she believes the land was God given to Israel and thus is to be claimed to the exclusion of any who resist. Her reasoning, however, is somewhat different; she traces her ancestry through Jews who have lived in Palestine since before the Romans. The Romans drove her ancestors from Jerusalem, but

---

*Population growth in Israel has been substantially dependent upon people immigrating to Israel to become citizens. The Law of Return allows anyone who is defined as "Jewish" or a relative of any Jewish citizen in Israel to come and receive immediate citizenship. Most of those who come to Israel as immmigrants stay in Israel.

On the other hand, should an Israeli citizen want to emigrate, to leave Israel to become a citizen of another country, then the rules of the country to which one wishes to go must be met. These rules vary greatly from country to country. There are large Jewish communities in a number of countries in the world (e.g. Argentina, Australia, Brazil, Canada, France, Great Britain, Hungary, Russia, South Africa, Uruguay), but the largest is in the United States.

To immigrate into the United States one can qualify in several ways, but the quickest route is to have relatives already here. The surest way is to be married to a U.S. citizen or to be the parent of a U.S. citizen. Having a profession or skill that is considered important to U.S. authorities is the second best way to gain entrance, but only a certain number of people can enter in any one year. In comparison to that of Great Britain and France, the United States' policy is more restrictive.

not out of Palestine. They moved to the Galilee, where they lived for centuries. Shortly after the 1973 war, Dvorah's parents returned to the outskirts of Jerusalem, where Dvorah was born. To Dvorah, the continual presence of Jews in Palestine is a testimony to God's promises. She is quick to share her family's history because, in her opinion, it establishes a prior claim to the land, superior to that of any "latecomers" among the Arab population. She believes that Jewish rights to the land are better established than those of the Palestinians by reason of the Bible and the ongoing Jewish presence in the land. Her current goal is to see all the territory that Israel has occupied since 1967 settled and established as Jewish. Arabs may or may not be welcome to live within this expanded Israel, depending on how they choose to relate to Israelis, but Israel's right to all the land west of the Jordan River is unquestioned in Dvorah's mind.

Yael is the mother of two. Her husband is a chemical engineer. A *sabra*, Yael grew up in the home of an ardent Zionist. During her childhood and early adulthood she accepted the nationalism (sometimes militarism) of her family with little thought. Now, however, at the age of forty-two, she has begun to have serious doubts about the tactics her government is employing, particularly in the Occupied Territories. The inconvenience and humiliation often imposed on the Arab population at the numerous military checkpoints scattered through the West Bank, which she has personally witnessed, seem to her unjust, and as such, inappropriate for a Jewish government to continue. She has begun to question the long-standing axiom in her own family and in the country that the only answer to violence is greater violence. She considers the tactics used in Gaza and in Lebanon to be excessive and unwarranted. She is tired of war and believes that women will probably have to take a stronger lead in bringing an end to the bloodshed, as did the pan-banging women in Argentina. Yael's is clearly a minority voice, but a growing number of women and men share her dismay and grief.

Moshe is an orthodox Jew. His long black coat, fur-lined hat, and *pieyot* (sidelocks) indicate the Eastern European origins of his particular group. He belongs to a very strict orthodox sect whose members live in a part of Jerusalem called Mea Shearim. Moshe prefers to speak Yiddish, a language derived from High German. He believes Hebrew should be used only in prayer and in reading the Bible. A desire to be near the Western Wall and other holy places drew Moshe to Jerusalem some thirty years ago. Now, at the age of sixty-two, he is convinced that the state of Israel is the result of human rebellion, the work of human hands. Because only the Messiah can rightly restore Israel and bring back the Jews dispersed around the world, Moshe and his group refuse to acknowledge the legitimacy of the state of Israel. In his own eyes, he lives here in Jerusalem as a Jew, not an Israeli. His hope for a homeland can be fulfilled only with the Messiah's coming. In the meantime, Moshe is more concerned with the desecration of the Sabbath by secular Jews than with the threats of hostile Arab governments.

For most of Israel's existence Ashkenazic Jews (like Moshe, whose roots are in Eastern Europe and Russia) constituted the majority Jewish segment of Israeli society. It is they who provided most of the nation's leaders. In terms of the overall population, however, their majority has declined over the decades. Sephardic Jews (those whose roots are in countries around the Mediterranean Sea) have immigrated to Israel in large numbers and now challenge the Ashkenazim for leadership. These Sephardic Jews share much with Arabs in terms of culture because most grew up in Arab countries. Their Arab-like appearance and customs evoke suspicions among the Ashkenazim. The Sephardim as a group are less educated and less skilled. They have experienced some discrimination as they have taken their place in Israeli society. In addition, they are largely secular Jews or are only minimally religious.

Yaacob is a Sephardic Jew born in Morocco. He came to Israel in 1965, in his late teens, and served in the military during the 1967 war. He is as fluent in Arabic as in Hebrew. Now in his late fifties, he works as a tour-bus driver, a relatively good job, though that sector of the economy has suffered tremendously during the last several years. Yaacob is conservative in his political outlook. He does not question Israel's right to be in Palestine and will fight to protect his country. He is not hostile to Arabs in general—he grew up with Arabs and appreciates much in their culture—but he is convinced that Israel must deal from a position of power with any Arab governments that threaten Israel. While Yaacob is not a religious man, he does have a deep sense of Jewish tradition and the behavior that goes with that tradition. He is grateful for the State of Israel and sees it as a place where Jews can live in freedom as Jews. He accepts without much reflection the idea that the Jews of today are the continuation of the Israelites of the Bible. Thus it is appropriate for them to be here in Jerusalem and elsewhere in this land. Before the uprisings in the Occupied Territories and the series of bombings in Jerusalem and elsewhere, Yaacob could conceive of an Israel where Jew and Arab could live together peacefully, sharing the land. Now he is not so certain.

Daniel, age thirty-one, came to Israel from Ethiopia. He does not come to Jerusalem often since he lives in the Galilee. Daniel's people were part of a Jewish enclave known as Beta Israel who practiced a pre-Talmudic form of Judaism. They left Ethiopia because of increasing pressure and persecution by a hostile government. At the age of ten, Daniel, with many other young boys, faced the almost certain fate of separation from his family and conscription into military service. He is grateful that he was one of the lucky ones whose family was rescued in Operation Moses. This rescue mission was carried out by Israel between November 18, 1984, and January 5, 1985, when the government of Ethiopia agreed to allow Jews to leave and move to Israel. Others of his people have come to Israel as part of another dramatic rescue mission known as Operation Solomon. This airlift began on May 24, 1991, and lasted thirty-six hours. At that time nearly fifteen thousand Ethiopian Jews were brought to Israel, nearly completing the evacuation of the Beta Israel community. Some two thousand remain, and efforts continue to secure their release. Life in Israel for Daniel and the many who have followed—there are now approximately thirty-six thousand Ethiopian Jews in Israel—has not been easy. He left a primarily agricultural, closely knit community that was almost primitive by modern standards and had to adjust to a new culture with a new language and new style of life. His people have experienced some degree of discrimination, but not the physical threats and violence they knew in Ethiopia. Daniel has done reasonably well as a day worker, and is steadily taking his place in Israel as a good and committed citizen. He will defend his new country in whatever ways he is asked.

Sasha, age forty-two, has been in Israel for some fifteen years. She came among the first wave of Russian immigrants in the early nineties. She and her family could take very little with them when they left to come to Israel. Now she and her husband, who is a doctor, and their four children occupy a small two-bedroom apartment in one of the new communities encircling Jerusalem. She is grateful to be in Israel and learned Hebrew quickly. Like the Jews who came some years earlier from Ethiopia, Sasha's family cannot be said to practice traditional Judaism. Though religious Jews consider her "secular," that in no way reflects her attitude toward life. It merely testifies to her having grown up in a country where she was not permitted to practice her religion. She has empathy for many of the immigrants who find it difficult to adjust to their new situation in Israel. In general, because of the housing needs her friends experience, she supports the idea of settlements in parts of the land that are occupied primarily by Arabs, even if this means disregarding Arab claims of ownership. She is somewhat afraid of most Arabs anyway, viewing them as potential terrorists.

The impact of the million or more Russian Jews who have moved into Israel during the past decade has been significant. The changes that these new residents have caused are seen in the effects on housing, health care, education, labor policies, and the political process. The Ashkenazim "majority status" is once again secure. But most of the Russian immigrants are secular, and some have openly voiced their desire to return to their former homeland. Their depth of commitment to the State of Israel, to the land of Israel, is yet to be tested, though most seem to have made a good transition.

STILL OTHER PEOPLES AND OTHER VOICES

Other groups live within Israel, but they are rarely seen at the gates of the Old City in Jerusalem. The Druse, whose first language is Arabic, live mostly in the northern districts of Israel and in the Golan Heights. In much larger numbers they are found in parts of Syria and Lebanon. The Druse have developed a religion that seems to combine elements of both Christianity and Islam, though details are shared only with the initiated. They tend to stay close to their home areas and are known as fierce fighters when it comes to protecting their own. Unlike Arabs (Israeli and non-Israeli), the Druse serve in the Israeli army and border police. The government of Israel has allowed the Druse a fair amount of autonomy. In return, the Druse have generally been good citizens of Israel. It is only in the Golan Heights, which belonged to Syria prior to 1967, where any problems seem to exist. The Druse who live in this area have strong cultural ties with the large number of Druse who live in Syria. These cultural ties are much stronger than the geopolitical divisions that separate the Syrian Druse from the Israeli Druse in the Golan Heights. Loyalties are tested whenever Israeli or Syrian ambitions force the Druse to decide for Israel or Syria at the expense of other Druse.

The Bedouin, another group, primarily inhabit the Negev in the south of Israel. They are Arabs, and most are Muslims. Their traditional lifestyle is radically different from that of most Israelis, whether Arab or Jew. The Bedouin culture is patriarchal and organized in tribes. Women are veiled, marriages are arranged, and girls do not attend school. Until recently, the tribes roamed the desert freely with fierce independence and ignored most nationalistic pronouncements. They came into conflict with other Arabs and Jews only when the nationalistic interests of others threatened their own tribal interests. Since 1967, however, Israeli policy has discouraged nomadic lifestyles. The Bedouin have found their movements restricted by the creation of new military bases, nature reserves, and settlements. Many of the younger Bedouin have never really known desert life, but work as day laborers in hotels, at construction sites, and so on. They resent the loss of a way of life that was dear to them. They feel that the Israeli government is treating them unjustly. They long not for a nation of their own, but rather for the right to move freely with their flocks and to preserve their lifestyle.

VITAL DIVERSITY AS THE NORM

From this montage of individuals and their views, what can we learn about Israel, about human rights and human hopes, about the significance of land? Is there a single message or many messages? Given the wide variety of individuals and ethnic groups within Israel, clearly a number of important positions deserve recognition.

Both Jews and Arabs know a love for land; many have a genuine attachment to the land. Their identities are tied up with the land on which they live or to which they desire to return. For most, however, this is not a matter of philosophy or theology, but a much more concrete reaction to the realities of life. They want land on which to live and work. Those who have a place are committed to keeping it. Those who are without are determined to remedy that situation.

This issue has another level. Many Arabs and Jews possess nationalistic hope and pride. Many Jews, even those who do not want to live in Israel, are deeply proud of Israel as a nation. It is the homeland for Jews, a place where Jews can be Jews in safety and with dignity. The nation was established by international law, won and defended by military victory, and developed through hard work. Some Israelis trace their lineage to Jews who lived in the land in Roman times and even earlier. Israelis who may not agree on anything else are unified in their determination to protect their homeland.

Arabs also possess nationalistic fervor but obviously of a different sort. The more militant want to return to a bygone time, by force if necessary, a time when Israel did not exist. This desire is unrealistic. Others hope for some measure of autonomy, expressed preferably by a new nation for Arabs fashioned out of the Occupied Territories and coexisting with Israel. Still others want only to be treated fairly and allowed to maintain their own culture with some independence. Basic to all of these notions is the fact that some Arab families, Muslim and Christian, have lived in Palestine for generations. Their sense of entitlement to the land is based on their tenure on it, and sometimes their actual legal title to it, and the conviction that the United Nations had no right to partition Palestine in the first place.

What is most striking, though, is that relatively few have a well-developed religious notion or theology about land. When asked about their relationship to and understanding of Israel, most Arabs and most Jews answer at a secular level and emphasize nationalism or personal goals and desires. For non-Israeli Christians, this usually comes as a surprise, because many Western Christians talk about Israel/Palestine as the Holy Land, the promised land, the land once given to ancient Israel and now restored by God to Jewish descendants of the first Israel. While some Israeli Jews express these sentiments, they do not do so as frequently or with the fervor Western Christians generally expect. Some use the religious and historical tradition to defend the establishment of a Jewish state in this particular place in the Middle East as opposed to some other part of the world, but the creation of the nation by the United Nations and the successful defense and development of the land are far more important to most Israelis than the religious claim.

Arab Muslims and Arab Christians usually reject any religious claim by Jews to the land. According to these Christians and Muslims, even if the land once was given to ancient Israel, it was lost because of disobedience. The ancient promise has no continuing value and certainly does not justify displacing Arabs in favor of Jews. Some Israeli Jews agree and disavow any religious claim on the land.

The rich diversity of people and opinion we have surveyed offers a brief, fundamental understanding of contemporary

Israel. No single view concerning land emerges as normative. Efforts to articulate a theological perspective about land must begin with an acknowledgment of Israel's pluralism. Many opinions are expressed and are worthy of consideration. Formulations based on religion have often been more hurtful than helpful. Nonetheless there is a religious, a theological, dimension to the talk about land that, though not paramount, should not be ignored. In bringing to expression this theological understanding, it is important to review the history of the people in the land of Israel. That will be the aim in chapter 2.

QUESTIONS FOR DISCUSSION

1. What are some of the opinions of the people described that surprised, disturbed, or delighted you? Why? In what ways?
2. What points of agreement, if any, can be found among these different points of view?
3. In what ways are the nationalistic and religious claims of Jews and Arabs concerning the land similar and different?
4. What are some of the reasons (negative and positive) for the author's contention in the final paragraph: "Formulations based on religion have often been more hurtful than helpful. Nonetheless there is a religious, a theological, dimension to the talk about land that, though not paramount, should not be ignored."

FOR FURTHER READING

Bailey, Betty Jane, and J. Martin Bailey. *Who Are the Christians in the Middle East?* Grand Rapids: Wm. B. Eerdmans, 2003.

Burrell, David, and Yehezkel Landau, eds. *Voices from Jerusalem*. Mahwah, NJ: Paulist Press, 1991.

Cragg, Kenneth. *The Arab Christian: A History in the Middle East.* Louisville, KY: Westminster/John Knox Press, 1991.

Friedman, Maurice. *Encounter on the Narrow Ridge: A Life of Martin Buber*. New York: Paragon House, 1991.

Golan-Agnon, Daphna. *Next Year in Jerusalem: Everyday Life in a Divided Land*. New York and London: New Press, 2005.

Raheb, Mitri. *I Am a Palestinian Christian*. Minneapolis: Fortress Press, 1995.

Sacks, Jonathan. *The Dignity of Difference*. London and New York: Continuum, 2002.

Shipler, David K. *Arab and Jew: Wounded Spirits in a Promised Land*. New York: Penguin Books, 1987.

2

The Realities of History

People, Power, and Palestine

The contemporary country of Israel is home to numerous people. Many have come from other places—from Europe, North Africa, the United States. They are drawn to Israel by religious motivation, the search for freedom and security, the hope of greater economic opportunity, and combinations of these motives as well as others. Many people have always lived there and trace their lineage in the land through many centuries. They live now in a country called Israel, but their ancestors knew it by other names. Native born, immigrants, refugees, victims of war, zealous settlers, cautious survivors, Jews, Muslims, Christians, secularists—they are all part of Israel and they ensure both vitality and conflict.

How this wide and rich variety of people come to be in Israel is important. Theological reflection apart from historical reality can foster grave misunderstanding if not outright error. Christians have all too often painted beautiful theological pictures while ignoring the harsh realities of time and place. Authentic theology requires serious and clear-sighted historical understanding. General theological statements about land may be formulated, but any application of these principles will always be particular, specific, and concrete, requiring historical understanding and judgment. In choosing to use contemporary Israel as a focus of a wider theological consideration, some historical review becomes necessary.

A survey of the history of postbiblical Palestine culminating with contemporary Israel is made all the more important because so much misunderstanding—indeed even ignorance—exists among North American Christians and others. Without some basic understanding of events, fair judgment—to say nothing of sympathy and compassion—is impossible. While Israel is often in the headlines, few readers seem to have bothered to acquaint themselves with the history that can put the headlines in proper perspective. Both bad theology and bad politics flourish when history is neglected or ignored.

To be sure, the writing of history is always biased to some degree. Writers inevitably make choices of what to include, which sources to use, and whom to believe or not believe. Absolutely "objective" historical reporting does not exist. No one—Christian, Jew, or Muslim—can be utterly neutral, but a level of fairness and accuracy can still be maintained. Fact and opinion are both important, and the way in which they are intertwined determines the trustworthiness and usefulness of a historical review. In this volume, I will discuss the legitimacy of the State of Israel's existence alongside the ambiguity and complexity of much of Israel's history. At the same time, I acknowledge Palestinian cries for justice as well founded, but I also note Arab culpability for many of the difficulties the Palestinians experience. Not every account would read this way. You, the reader, must judge the fairness and adequacy of the material.

The realities of our world situation affect our theological judgments. Conclusions suited for one situation may not fit another. The challenge of faith is to put the abstract formulations of theology into practical use, to live out what is preached. Thus, a brief review of the history of postbiblical Palestine culminating with modern-day Israel is in order.

THE IMPACT OF ROME

The Roman siege had lasted for months. Within Jerusalem, competing groups of Jews had often clashed in the struggle to lead the resistance. When the walls were finally breached in 70 CE and the enemy stormed into the city, the horrors of war reached a climax. As the Jewish historian Josephus recounts in *Wars of the Jews* (6.5), written between 80 and 90 CE:

> While the holy house was on fire, everything was plundered that came to hand, and ten thousand of those that were caught were slain; nor was there a commiseration of any age, or any reverence of gravity; but children, and old men, and profane persons, and priests, were all slain in the same manner; so that this war went round all sorts of men, and brought them to destruction, and as well those that made supplication for their lives, as those that defended themselves by fighting. The flame was also carried a long way, and made an echo, together with the groans of those that were slain; and because this hill was high, and the works at the temple were very great, one would have thought that the whole city had been on fire. Nor can one imagine anything either greater or more terrible than this noise; for there was at once a shout of the Roman legions, who were marching all together, and a sad clamour of the seditious, who were now surrounded with fire and sword.

Thus, military and civilian, combatants and noncombatants, were slaughtered. The carnage was frightful. Fortifications, governmental quarters, the Temple—all were destroyed! Only a portion of the western wall of Herod's Temple, which centuries later became revered as the "Wailing Wall," survived. The Judean revolt was over. A new era began.

THE DISPERSION

So it was that the Roman army under Titus overpowered and subdued Jerusalem in 70 CE. The revolt had begun four years earlier. Roman response was immediate and brutal. The countryside was subdued first, and then the legions turned to Jerusalem, the symbol of religious and political independence. The Romans, by slaughtering the people and destroying the capital, inaugurated what has come to be known as the Diaspora, or dispersion, of the Jews throughout the Roman Empire and eventually beyond. Centuries earlier (587 BCE) the Babylonians under Nebuchadnezzar had dealt with rebellion in a similar manner, leveling Jerusalem (and many of the neighboring towns and villages) and taking the leadership of the city and nation into exile. The Jews who escaped the ravages of the Roman conqueror in 70 CE were forbidden to rebuild Jerusalem. They left the city to take up life elsewhere, in the Galilee, and in Syria, Egypt, and other places around the Mediterranean Sea.

Power—brutal physical power—has often defined the political realities of Palestine. From antiquity, people in the Middle East have brutalized one another. Memories of oppression and subjugation are nourished and preserved for decades, for centuries. The Jews of the Diaspora never forgot that a merciless enemy stripped them of their political and religious independence and sent them into exile. Centuries passed with Jews all around the world remembering and praying for a day when they might once again return to the land of their historical beginnings and to Jerusalem. The plea and promise repeated in every Passover Seder—Next year in Jerusalem!—never lost its meaning.

PALESTINE

The land itself was given a "political" name, Palestine. The forebears of the Jews expelled from Jerusalem in 70 CE, had known the area as Judea. The Old Testament regularly names this territory the "land of Canaan." Later Jews know this land as *Eretz Yisrael,* the land of Israel. But the Bible never refers to this variously occupied territory as "Palestine."

The name "Palestine" is derived from the name of one of ancient Israel's early enemies, the Philistines, who settled on the southern coast of Canaan. Herodotus, an ancient Greek historian, was apparently the first to use the word "Palestine," a Greek form of "Philistia," which was the territory of the Philistines, as a designation for the area. After the attempted revolt of the Jewish nationalist Bar-Kochba against Rome in 135 CE, the Roman emperor Hadrian removed the name "Province of Judea" from official records and monuments and used the name "Province of Syria Palestine" or simply "Palestine" in its place. Thus, Palestine became the region's name largely to punish the Jews and to remind them that they no longer controlled or had a claim to this territory.

Later, three provinces had the name *Palaestina*. Two were primarily west of the Jordan River (*Palaestina prima* and *Palaestina secunda*), and one was south and east (*Palaestina tertia*). Most of the area designated by some form of the term "Palestine" was in Cisjordan (west of the Jordan), but some was in Transjordan (east of the Jordan). In the modern era, following World War I, the British revived the term Palestine for the land west of the Jordan (Cisjordan), which was under their rule. In 1923 they also created an emirate under their control in Transjordon, east of the Jordan River, now known as Jordan.

Today's difficulties over the land are all the more complex because, as early as the second century of the Common Era, the term "Palestine" designated the whole area now divided into Israel, Jordan, Lebanon, and Syria. Different people, depending on time, place, and political commitment, can mean, and have meant, different things when using the term. It is enough for us to remember that it is a term that was forcibly imposed, at least in part, for political reasons, as a denial of Judean-Jewish claims on the territory.

THE BYZANTINE ERA

Following the Romans, many rulers exercised political and military power over Palestine. Under Constantine the Great (324 CE), Christianity became the established religion of the newly

revived and reunited Roman Empire, and the Byzantine period
began. Basically Christians exercised hegemony over Palestine,
the Holy Land. Numerous holy places were identified and
became the destination for Christian pilgrims. Jews were allowed
limited access to Jerusalem, but only on the anniversary of the
destruction of the Temple, the ninth of Av. At times during the
years of Byzantine rule, conflicts broke out between the Christian rulers and various Jews and Samaritans seeking independence (484, 526–65 CE).

In 614 CE, the Persians conquered Palestine, and some
thirty-seven thousand Christians were taken prisoner to Persia.
For fourteen years, Persia allowed Jews to rule Jerusalem again.
The Christians who remained were given the choice of renounc-
ing their faith or being killed. Power and politics at the service
of religion continued to be the norm.

ARAB RULE BEGINS

Muhammad, the founder of the Islamic religion, was born
around 570 CE. He is called the Prophet of Islam, and there
are three spellings of his name: Muhammad, Mohammed, and
Mahomet. By 632 CE, when Muhammad died, Islam had
spread throughout most of the Arabian Peninsula. Subsequently,
the Muslims conquered the whole area that included the modern countries of Egypt, Iraq, Israel, Jordan, Lebanon, and Syria
and eventually extended their empire as far west as Spain and as
far east as India. The capital of the empire was placed in Damascus, Syria, in 661 CE. Arab rule of Jerusalem and Palestine was
part of the conquest that began shortly after Muhammad died,
and it was firmly established in Jerusalem by 638 CE.

Shortly after 1000 CE, radical Muslim leaders began to
persecute non-Muslims in Palestine, particularly Christians.
The Church of the Holy Sepulchre in Jerusalem was destroyed
in 1009. The brutality encountered during the next several
decades by Christians within Palestine and by pilgrims seeking
to visit the Holy Land was one justification for the Crusades.

THE CRUSADES

Between 1099 and 1291, at least seven Crusades were launched by Christians in Europe to deliver the Holy Land from the hands of the infidels, namely the Muslims. Atrocity was not limited to one side in these fierce conflicts, but Christians especially showed little understanding or discrimination in their attacks. Jews and Muslims, civilians and combatants, were often slaughtered indiscriminately by the crusaders in the name of God and for the purpose of reclaiming control over the holy places sacred to Christian tradition. Eventually, however, the Christian crusaders were repelled and Muslim rule resumed.

Around 1250 the Mamelukes, Muslims who came to power in Egypt, extended their authority into Palestine after the crusaders were ejected. During the next two and a half centuries under Mameluke rule considerable building occurred in the area. In 1492, Jews and Muslims were expelled from Spain, and many went east to a welcoming Palestine.

THE OTTOMAN EMPIRE

In 1517, Sultan Selim I, a Turkish Muslim leader, captured Jerusalem. Palestine thereby became part of the Ottoman Empire, which extended across North Africa, to the south to Yemen, and through Greece to Hungary. Under Selim's son, Suleiman the Magnificent, new walls were built around Jerusalem, and those walls still surround the Old City. Turkish law became well established and still is a factor in some disputes between Israelis and Palestinians. Ottoman rule extended for four centuries, and was too often marred by exploitation of natural resources, political mismanagement, and corruption. Toward the end of the Ottoman period, in response to the misrule and to protect their people and interests, various European nations established special agreements with a number of particular communities (especially Christians) living in Palestine and thereby became their patrons.

In World War I, the Ottoman Empire was allied with Germany. When Germany was defeated, the Ottoman Empire also was ended. Between 1917 and 1918 the British established a military administration. Then, in 1920 the League of Nations, in the style of the colonialism of the preceding century, placed Palestine (i.e., the territory that now is Israel and Jordan) under British mandate and Syria (including modern Lebanon) under French mandate. The British mandate lasted through World War II and expired on May 15, 1948. This was a tumultuous period and directly influenced the events of the most recent fifty-eight years. Osama ben Laden, the leader of the international Islamic resistance movement Al-Qaeda, for instance, has based his attacks on the West, in part at least, as a protest against the dismantling of the Ottoman Empire that ended Muslim hegemony in the region.

MODERN ZIONISM

Our historical survey must pause and step back to consider one of the most significant movements to affect the history of the Middle East in the modern era. In 1882 a new impulse of attention to Palestine began. The first of several great waves of Jewish immigration to Palestine occurred, largely in reaction to oppression in Russia and Poland. A group called "Hovevei-Zion" (Lovers of Zion) spurred this first *aliyah*—a term literally translated "going up" but meaning "arrival" in the area now known as Israel. This was the beginning of "practical Zionism," which aimed at establishing Jewish settlements in Palestine.

Shortly thereafter, in 1896, Theodor Herzl, an Austrian Jew who was both journalist and playwright, launched "political Zionism" with the publication of his book *Jewish State*. Herzl called for the creation of a Jewish national home in Palestine. His proposal was prompted by the desperation he and other Jews felt as anti-Jewish feeling and discriminatory laws quickened across Europe.

Herzl's thinking was galvanized by the conviction of French army officer Alfred Dreyfus on trumped-up treason charges in 1894. Dreyfus, a Jew, was a victim of the anti-Jewish sentiment rampant in the army and elsewhere in French society. Although Dreyfus was fully exonerated after years of imprisonment, the affair was most sobering to Herzl. France might have been more progressive than other European nations, Herzl reasoned, but if Dreyfus could be so ill-treated in France, then nowhere in Europe could Jews be confident of enjoying full, first-class citizenship.

Therefore, Herzl dreamed of gathering Jews from around the world, and especially from Europe, to create a Jewish nation. His motive was political, not religious. The remedy for anti-Jewish repression was to create an independent Jewish nation where Jews could live safely while enjoying and perpetuating their culture. Herzl began his movement of political Zionism with the goal of attaining political recognition of a Jewish homeland.

In 1897, the First Zionist Congress was held in Basel, Switzerland, and a worldwide movement was organized to attract support for the right to a Jewish state. The goal was "to create for the Jewish people a home in Palestine secured by public law." Herzl died in 1904 and thus saw little fruit of his labors, but a movement had begun.

A revival of Hebrew as a spoken and literary language began during the last years of the nineteenth century, and Zionism encouraged this revival. Poetry, essays, and novels appeared, and a dictionary was produced. As Zionism proceeded, Hebrew became its language.

Practical Zionism remained primary until after World War I. From 1904 to 1914 a second major wave of Jewish immigration from Europe, the second aliyah, was organized. By 1914 nearly one hundred thousand Jews had settled in Palestine, alongside approximately six hundred thousand Arabs. In 1909 Tel Aviv was established as a purely Jewish city. Around 1910 the first kibbutz (a collective community) was organized. A vital, energized Jewish presence was thus firmly rooted in Palestine, complementing the smaller communities of Jews who had never left the area.

Political Zionism took on new significance during World War I. After conquering Palestine, Great Britain pledged support for a Jewish national homeland in the Balfour Declaration of 1917. The statement was issued by British Foreign Secretary Arthur James Balfour as a part of an effort to gain Jewish support for Britain's campaign to control the Suez Canal. The declaration read:

> His Majesty's Government view with favour the establishment in Palestine of a national home for the Jewish people, and will use their best endeavors to facilitate the achievement of this object, it being clearly understood that nothing shall be done which may prejudice the civil and religious rights of existing non-Jewish communities in Palestine, or the rights and political status enjoyed by Jews in any other country.

This statement was endorsed by the League of Nations in 1922. Britain's mandate over Palestine was reaffirmed, but in 1923 the territory that now is Jordan was removed from the mandate.

The Balfour Declaration gave great impetus to political Zionism's goal of creating a Jewish homeland in Palestine. An organization called the Jewish Agency was recognized by Britain as the representative of Jews in Palestine. Cultural, educational, and economic institutions were created, and immigration was encouraged. Ever-increasing numbers of Jews came to Palestine, particularly after 1933, as the shadow of an anti-Jewish Third Reich grew longer. The exact numbers are much debated and are difficult to determine because of the way the records were kept, but the number of Jews grew dramatically.

Zionists interpreted the Balfour Declaration and the subsequent League of Nations mandate as a clear indication of Britain's intention and obligation to assist in the creation of an independent Jewish state. But others—including, as time went on, the British—did not see it that way. The British originally planned to create self-governing institutions for each of the various peoples settled in Palestine, including the large Arab majority. Arab leaders interpreted the declaration to mean that a Jewish state in Palestine could be established only if Arabs agreed to it. During the 1920s and 1930s, a number of Arab riots directed against Jews occurred as an expression of Arab opposition to establishing a Jewish homeland in Palestine.

Open rebellion by the Arabs against British rule began in 1936. For the next several years, efforts at compromise were made. Britain recommended in the Peel Report that Palestine be partitioned between Arabs and Jews, but the Arabs rejected this plan. In an effort to end the rebellion and to gain much-needed Arab support as the international situation deteriorated toward war, Britain decided in 1939 to limit the creation of Jewish settlements and to end all Jewish immigration to Palestine for five years.

This action eventually proved Britain's undoing in the region. At the very moment when Jews most needed a safe place to which to flee from a well-orchestrated and well-organized campaign of genocide, the British closed the door to Palestine. Zionists and many other Jews were outraged. For the Arabs, it was too little too late. Britain's mandate did not end until 1948, but the troubles seen in the 1920s and 1930s would only increase.

It is important to note that not all Arabs were against all Jews. In numerous cases, Jews and Arabs lived peaceably side-by-side in cooperation and mutual respect, with each knowing the other's language. The politics of national states did not control these relationships.

Moreover, then as now, not all Jews were Zionists. Some Jews living in Palestine, as well as in Europe and the United States, rejected political Zionism on the grounds that only God could restore Jews to their homeland and would do so in God's time—not on some human time schedule. Some also insisted that Jews were a religious community and not a nationality. They did not view the establishment of a Jewish state as a religious obligation at all. They were not necessarily against the aims of Zionism, but they saw no reason to endorse them either. A Jewish homeland in Palestine was not a first priority.

THE DIVISION OF PALESTINE

During World War II (1939–45), Arab and Jewish resistance to British rule was at a minimum. A greater threat was recognized, and many Palestinian Arabs and Jews joined the Allies in the struggle against the Axis powers. (A notorious exception was Mohammed Said Haj Amin el Husseini, who as mufti of Jerusalem was spiritual leader of Jerusalem's Muslim community and actively supported Adolf Hitler.) With the war's end, however, attention again turned to Palestine. Britain continued to limit Jewish immigration severely. The situation for Jews in Europe remained terrible. After the horror of the Holocaust, displaced Jews needed a place to go immediately. Desperate times fostered desperate action: Jews organized resistance—terrorism, opponents would call it—against British authorities and installations. One of the most dramatic acts was the demolition of a wing of the famous King David Hotel in Jerusalem, then being used as the administrative headquarters of the British military forces.

Britain took the matter to the United Nations in 1947, and the U.N. Special Commission on Palestine was established. This commission recommended that Palestine be divided into an Arab state and a Jewish state, with Jerusalem under international control and open to all. The proposed boundaries are shown on the map titled "U.N. Partition Plan." After much debate, the United Nations adopted this plan on November 29, 1947. The Jews quickly accepted the proposal, but the Arabs refused, arguing that the United Nations had no right to give away land that belonged to them. Hostilities broke out within Palestine but, more significantly, the Arab nations surrounding the disputed area vowed a war to drive the Jews out of the land and began preparations for it.

The British mandate was scheduled to expire on May 15, 1948. On May 14, Palestinian Jews, led by David Ben-Gurion,

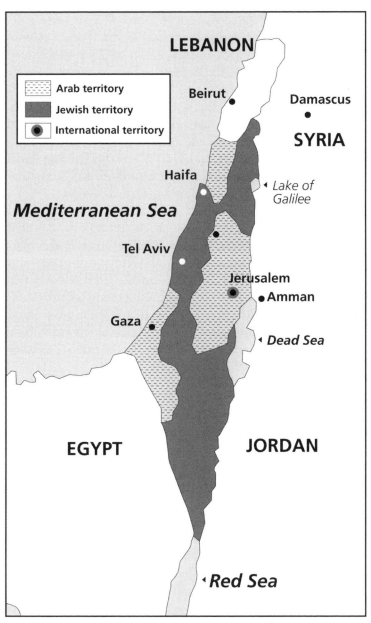

Map 1: U.N. Partition Plan

proclaimed an independent State of Israel. The next day, as the British completed their withdrawal, Egypt, Iraq, Lebanon, Syria, and Jordan (known as Transjordan until 1949) mustered troops to support Palestinian Arab efforts to extinguish the newly proclaimed Jewish state. The Arabs had a tremendous military advantage over the much smaller, poorly equipped Jewish forces, but they lacked a unified command. Some Arab units were never deployed, and early opportunities to overrun Jewish positions were squandered. When the fighting ended months later, the Jews somehow had prevailed. The modern State of Israel had survived its first critical challenge.

In the course of the conflict some seven hundred thousand Arabs were displaced. Many fled their homes out of fear of atrocity—rumored or real—at the hands of some Jewish fighters. Others anticipated a quick Arab victory and expected to return when the fighting was over. Instead, these refugees were to begin a long sojourn in neighboring Arab countries. For many of their children, grandchildren, and even great grandchildren, the exile continues. What Israelis came to call "Independence Day" was a day of mourning for the Arabs, a day now known as *el-Nakba,* "the Catastrophe."

At the conclusion of the fighting, Israel controlled—in addition to land designated for the Jewish state under the United Nations plan—the western half of Jerusalem and about half of the land designated by the United Nations for Arab control. This is shown on the map titled "Israel after 1948–49 War." Egypt and Jordan controlled the rest of the territory that had been known as Palestine under the partition plan. Those areas came to be called the West Bank (Jordanian territory west of the Jordan River) and the Gaza Strip (the area around Gaza on the Mediterranean coast, about forty-five miles south of Tel Aviv, which was controlled by Egypt).

On January 15, 1949, the United Nations negotiated a number of armistices to establish peace. The borders were drawn along the cease-fire line but were not recognized by the Arabs. Israel elected its first government, with Chaim Weizmann as president and David Ben-Gurion as prime minister.

Map 2: Israel after 1948-49 War

The first census taken by Israel of its population in 1948 recorded approximately 872,000 citizens, a number that included about 150,000 Arabs who had not fled at the outbreak of the fighting. Power and politics had once again rearranged the political geography of Palestine. A new nation, Israel, proclaimed as a homeland for Jews who had been scattered across the face of the globe for almost two millennia, took its place in world politics.

SECURING THE BORDERS

The early years of modern Israel's existence were difficult. Thousands of immigrants arrived and had to be settled; an economy had to be built. Without the assistance of the governments of the United States, Great Britain, and West Germany, in particular, and the contributions of Jewish communities and individuals from around the world, Israel could not have survived.

In addition to the stress of establishing the nation in an area with few natural resources and a limited work force, the reality of hostile neighbors and no readily defensible borders confronted Israel. Armed attackers could easily penetrate Israel's borders and did so frequently.

Matters came to a head in 1956. For several years, Egypt had been supporting attacks on Israel from the Gaza Strip, and Israel responded in kind. Because Israeli shipping was not allowed to pass through the Suez Canal, Israel had developed Eilat as its seaport on the Gulf of Aqaba, the northeast arm of the Red Sea. Egyptian artillery easily controlled the entrance to the gulf, however, and posed a threat to ships bound to or from Israel. In July 1956, Egypt seized the Suez Canal from the British and French who then controlled it, thus tightening the screws on Israel's economy.

On October 29, 1956, Israel invaded Egypt. The English and French, as prearranged, joined the fray in a very limited way and reclaimed the Suez Canal. Israel's army and air force soon overcame all other Egyptian resistance. By November 5, Israel's forces occupied the Gaza Strip and the Sinai Peninsula and had opened the Suez Canal and Gulf of Aqaba to Israeli shipping. The United Nations arranged cease-fires and assigned U.N. troops to maintain them. Israel withdrew its forces but had demonstrated its ability to defend its borders with military power.

Eleven years later, border violations once again precipitated a full-blown conflict. The United Nations had been able to reduce drastically the incursions along the Egyptian-Israeli border, but attacks and counterattacks along the borders between Israel and Syria and Israel and Jordan became steadily more frequent and destructive. The rhetoric of war, punctuated by armed clashes, reached a peak in 1967. Arab newspapers and radio stations clamored for a war of annihilation against Israel. Israel, and many of its supporters in the United States, feared for the nation's survival.

In May 1967, Egypt's President Gamal Abdel Nasser declared a blockade of Israeli shipping and prohibited strategic materials on non-Israeli vessels from the Straits of Tiran, which control access to Eilat. Israel tried diplomatic means to lift the blockade, but to no avail, and on June 5, 1967, Israeli planes launched a surprise attack on several critical airfields in Syria, Jordan, and Egypt. Within hours, Israel had nearly destroyed the Arab nations' air power. Fighting in this brief conflict, known as the Six-Day War, was fierce. By June 10, Israeli troops had occupied the Gaza Strip, the Sinai Peninsula up to the Suez Canal, Jordanian territory west of the Jordan River, and Syria's Golan Heights. Israel immediately proclaimed East Jerusalem, controlled by Jordan since the 1948 conflict, to be a part of Israel.

At the cease-fire, Israel held territory equal to three times its size before the war, as shown in the map titled "Israel and the Occupied Territories after the 1967 War." Thousands of people fled from East Jerusalem and the West Bank, mostly to Jordan and Syria. The Arab refugee population in these countries was greatly expanded. The Arab countries to which they fled did not assimilate them, restricting them mainly to overcrowded, poorly equipped camps. The Palestine Liberation Organization, then the leading political voice of the Palestinian Arab

Map 3: Israel and the Occupied Territories after the 1967 War

population, became committed to regaining the thousands of homesteads abandoned in the flight before the advancing Israelis. U.N. Resolution 242, passed on November 22, 1967, called for a return to prewar boundaries and the recognition by all parties of the rights of each other, including Israel, to exist in secure borders and at peace. More than a quarter century would pass before the first significant steps would be taken in 1993 toward fulfilling the latter part of the resolution.

By 1973 tension once again reached an intolerable level. Border fighting exploded into all-out war on October 6, when Egypt and Syria launched simultaneous attacks on Israel. The date was Yom Kippur, the Jewish Day of Atonement, and the most important of Jewish holidays. Fierce fighting and heavy casualties occurred in the Sinai Peninsula and the Golan Heights. In November 1973, Israel and Egypt agreed to a cease-fire, but the fighting between Syria and Israel continued until June 1974. Israel had penetrated both Egyptian and Syrian territory but agreed to withdraw to prewar borders. A buffer zone along the Suez Canal and in the Golan Heights, patrolled by U.N. forces, was established.

THE CAMP DAVID ACCORDS

Israel had once again proved able to defend its borders, but at heavy cost. The Yom Kippur War, as this conflict was called, clearly demonstrated Israel's military prowess, but it also revealed much unrest in the nation. Israelis had not experienced the level of casualties in either the 1956 Suez War or the 1967 Six-Day War that they suffered in the Yom Kippur War. The government's handling of events prior to and during the conflict was criticized. Golda Meir, who had been prime minister since 1969, resigned in 1974. The economy was under great pressure. Three years later, in 1977, the Labor Party, which had controlled the government since independence, was ousted in favor of the Likud Party.

The new government, under the leadership of Prime Minister Menachem Begin, immediately began to seek political resolution of disputes with its neighbors. Anwar el Sadat of Egypt responded. Eventually, through the mediation of U.S. President Jimmy Carter, Begin and Sadat signed the Camp David Accords. A peace treaty between Egypt and Israel was signed on March 26, 1979, and Israel began a withdrawal from the Sinai Peninsula that was completed in 1982.

One important provision of the Camp David Accords was never accomplished. Self-government for the Gaza Strip and West Bank was to have been established for five years, after which a final decision was to be made on their status. Details could not be agreed upon, however. On July 30, 1980, Israel declared Jerusalem to be "capital of Israel for all time," an action still not recognized by the United States. In 1981, Israel announced the formal annexation of East Jerusalem and the Golan Heights, which it had occupied since 1967. The West Bank and Gaza continued under military rule.

THE PALESTINE LIBERATION ORGANIZATION

At the end of Israel's 1948 War of Independence, approximately seven hundred thousand Arabs who had previously resided in territory claimed by the new state were living in Arab countries, principally Lebanon, Syria, Jordan, and Egypt. These refugees had one overriding goal: to return to their homes. Of course, this required that Israel be eliminated. Unrest and hate of Israel filled the camps where these thousands of displaced Arabs lived. The major Arab governments did not try seriously to assimilate these people or do much to alleviate the squalid conditions in which many lived. Rather, they chose to use the refugees as pawns in their designs against Israel.

In 1964, the Arab heads of state created the Palestine Liberation Organization (PLO) as a way of controlling the Palestinians living in their countries. The charter of the PLO, written in Cairo, refused to acknowledge Israel as a legitimate state. It declared that the land of Palestine was Arab land and the Jews had no right to any part of it. The charter pledged unending hostility against Israel until all Arab land was restored to its true owners. The Jews would be driven out so that Arabs could return.

As events unfolded during the 1950s and 1960s, the PLO's goals seemed less and less realistic. Israel was clearly able to defend itself. Prior to the 1967 Six-Day War, most Arab refugees were from areas within the borders that Israel had established in 1948. To return to these places was not possible without the destruction of Israel, and each war made that seem less likely.

Even before the PLO was created, groups had been formed for the purpose of liberating Palestine. One of the first was al-Fatah (Victory), created in Kuwait in 1956 by a group of middle-class Palestinians whose spokesman was Mohammed "Yasir" (a nickname meaning "easy" that was given him as a child) Arafat. Al-Fatah carried out numerous attacks on Israel during the 1960s. Although other groups existed, Arafat's organization was the most successful and best known.

Arafat's reputation grew, and in 1969 he was able to gain control of the PLO from the Arab governments. He turned it into an organization truly concerned with the Palestinian cause. In 1974 the Arab governments acknowledged the PLO as the "sole, legitimate representative of the Palestinian people"; the United Nations also recognized the PLO that year. Israel, not surprisingly, refused to recognize or deal with the PLO and maintained this stance until secret negotiations, which began early in 1993, culminated with the mutual recognition of Israel and the PLO.

Under Arafat the PLO became an organization with considerable power. Arab governments contributed large amounts of money to it annually, and the PLO developed a multi-billion-dollar investment portfolio that generated more than $200 million a year for the PLO's operating budget. Radio stations, newspapers, educational programs, scholarships, health payments, diplomatic missions, weapon purchases—all were made possible through the PLO. Indeed, some sixty thousand Palestinian families were directly dependent upon the PLO for their well-being.

THE INVASION OF LEBANON

During the 1970s, the PLO had its base of operations in Beirut, Lebanon. Jordan's King Hussein drove the PLO militia from Jordan in 1970 (because their raids against Israel led to Israeli retaliation against Jordan), and as a result, Syria and Lebanon saw a great influx of Palestinians. Tensions moderated between Jordan and Israel considerably, but not between Lebanon and Israel. Lebanon's civil war was beginning in 1975 and generated further difficulties for Israel because no authority was able to prevent attacks from across the Lebanese border. PLO military units situated in Lebanon acted with complete freedom to strike against Israel.

On June 6, 1982, Israel invaded Lebanon, with the goal of annihilating the PLO. Within a week, the Israeli army reached Beirut and besieged it. In the following months, Arafat reluctantly signed a declaration that included an acknowledgment of Israel's right to exist. In exchange, remnants of the PLO forces were evacuated from Beirut to Tunis that August. The PLO had not been eradicated, but certainly the organization's power had been greatly curtailed.

The Israeli army eventually was largely withdrawn from Lebanon in 1985, but it maintained a partial presence, as indicated on the map titled "Israel's Borders as of 1985." During the occupation, several events both memorable and horrible took place. In September 1982, with Israeli army units providing cover, Lebanese Christian militiamen entered two Palestinian refugee camps, Sabra and Shatila, and mercilessly slaughtered hundreds of people. The victims were mostly women and children. When news of this horror reached Israel, four hundred thousand Israelis demonstrated in Tel Aviv on September 24 to demand the resignation of the government and prosecution of those directly responsible for the massacre.

The other event illustrates the chaotic and brutal situation in Beirut during Israel's occupation of Lebanon. U.S. Marines arrived in August 1982 to stabilize the situation and support the government then in power. The Marines' movements and

Map 4: Israel's Borders as of 1985

authority were greatly restricted, and while the Lebanese initially received the Marines enthusiastically, eventually they became identified with "one side." The climax came on October 23, 1983, when a truck carrying twelve thousand pounds of dynamite was driven into the Marine headquarters, where it exploded, killing 241 U.S. soldiers who were acting as peacekeepers. In February 1984, President Reagan withdrew the Marines.

Many Israelis regarded the invasion of Lebanon as a costly mistake. The government that planned and carried it out was forced out of office, with Defense Minister Ariel Sharon resigning on February 2, 1983, and Prime Minister Begin on September 9, 1983. While Israel's goal of securing the border of Lebanon could be understood, the invasion went well beyond that. Initially a military victory, the invasion was a political disaster. The Israeli populace was angered and embarrassed. Moreover, support for Israel in the United States dropped significantly because of the massacres at Sabra and Shatila. And after the Beirut bombing of the Marines, many Americans were ready to get out of the Middle East altogether.

The slaughter in the refugee camps had an unexpected effect on the people living under military rule in the West Bank and Gaza Strip. The PLO had left the civilians in the camps unprotected, and it had withdrawn from Lebanon. West Bank and Gaza Strip Palestinians came to realize that, with the humiliation of the PLO military, they could count on no one but themselves.

As a result of Israel's invasion of Lebanon, an even more dedicated Palestinian nationalism took root among the Arab population. Some Muslim clerics came together in Lebanon and formed Hezbollah, the Party of God. The original purpose of this Islamic group was armed resistance to the Israeli occupation. Hezbollah carried out the bombing of the Marine headquarters, for instance, and conducted numerous guerrilla-style attacks against Israeli troops. Across the years Hezbollah widened its mission and became an active participant in Lebanon's political process. Further, it established an effective welfare program aimed at benefiting the 40 percent Muslim (largely Shia) population of Lebanon situated in the southern section of the country. Hezbollah, supported heavily by Syria and Iran, replaced Arafat's Fatah as the representative of the Palestinians in Lebanon and incorporated into its mission the elimination of Israeli occupation in all of Lebanon and all of Palestine, that is, the elimination of Israel as a state.

THE UPRISING

Four days in December 1987 produced a profound change in the relation between Israel and the million-plus Arabs who lived in the West Bank and Gaza Strip. First, on December 6, a Palestinian in Gaza fatally stabbed an Israeli shopper named Shlomo Sakle. Then, on December 8, an Israeli truck killed four Palestinian workers from the Jabaliya refugee camp in Gaza and injured seven others; Palestinians were convinced it was intentional, while Israeli police concluded it was an accident. On the following day, an unruly Palestinian protest ended with Israeli soldiers killing a seventeen-year-old Palestinian boy, Hatem Abu Sisi. Like a match to tinder, these events touched off the uprising (in Arabic, the *intifada*). The protest that erupted in the Jabaliya camp quickly spread throughout the West Bank. On December 21, the seven hundred thousand Arabs who were Israeli citizens mounted a solidarity strike. The anger that had been smoldering and building during twenty years of military occupation in Gaza and the West Bank was released. Things would not be the same again.

The intifada surprised everyone. The Israelis could not at first believe it was a genuine, internally led uprising. They tried to blame it on outsiders. They tried to deny its wide support. But it continued unabated. The more the military tried to enforce cooperation, the less it achieved. Some have argued that the Israeli authorities showed restraint, and it is true that the best-equipped military in the Middle East could have inflicted far more damage had it been allowed or encouraged to do so. Amnesty International reported that in 1992 Palestinians killed more than 200 of their own people who were suspected of being collaborators, while Israeli forces killed only 120. Nonetheless, despite such statistics, the Arab population, particularly the young, suffered far too many deaths and injuries as an ever more frustrated Israeli military tried unsuccessfully to break the resistance. And more and more Israelis clearly began to question the economic, human, and moral costs of continuing the conflict.

The intifada also surprised the Arab world outside Palestine, particularly the PLO. No one expected the Palestinians in the Gaza Strip and the West Bank to take their future into their own hands. The PLO had no role in launching or leading the uprising. In November 1988, nearly a year after the intifada began, the Palestine National Council (the PLO's parliament in exile) acted to support the uprising by declaring an independent Palestinian state, though borders were not drawn.

The intifada probably surprised the Palestinians in the Gaza Strip and West Bank most of all. For twenty years they had talked a lot but done little. Individuals had occasionally resisted, but not communities. Palestinians had talked of being a people but had not mobilized. Then, almost overnight, Palestinian consciousness and unity took a giant step forward. The resistance was actually quite controlled. Rocks can and did inflict fatal injuries, but the stones did not fare well as a rival for automatic weapon fire. The economic shutdowns and the orchestrated rock-throwing incidents that marked the intifada as it moved through its second year were designed more to build a sense of unity within the Palestinian community than to inflict serious injury on Israel. By rising up as they did, the Palestinians living under Israeli military occupation said: "No more! We are a people!"

Certainly related to the resistance in Gaza and the West Bank was the adoption of the Palestine Declaration of Independence. This document implicitly recognized Israel's right to exist in peace and security, an acknowledgment Arafat made explicit on December 14, 1988. Though the PLO Charter has yet to be officially altered to reflect such a change in policy, it nonetheless signaled a new perspective. Some forty years after a war intended to annihilate the Jewish state, this Arab group had in effect accepted the U.N. 1947 partition plan and the subsequent U.N. Resolutions 242 and 338, which called all parties to acknowledge the others' right to a secure state with peace.

THE SETTLEMENTS

The situation was complicated by the policy of the Likud Party under the leadership of Yitzhak Shamir. In response to the intifada, Shamir stepped up the creation of Jewish settlements within the Occupied Territories. The West Bank became routinely called Judea and Samaria (biblical names) by many Israelis, implying that this area was to be viewed as belonging to modern Israel, as it had to ancient Israel. The Jewish settlements and outposts were placed strategically throughout Judea and Samaria (especially around Jerusalem) and in Gaza in the midst of a largely hostile Palestinian population, usually on land that had been understood as Palestinian land.

While the outposts often consisted of only a few trailers surrounded by barbed wire fences with a few dozen occupants, the settlements usually had well-built housing for several thousand, even tens of thousands, settlers. They were self-contained small towns. Further, over the years a large network of bypass roads was developed in the West Bank to connect the settlements. These roads effectively divided the territory into grids, often separating Arab villages from Arab grazing pastures and farmland. The use of these roads is severely restricted to the Jewish settlers, and only a very few Palestinians are given access.

The number of these settlements and outposts reached a peak in early 2005 with over three hundred established, housing some four hundred thousand settlers. The number has diminished some with Israel's withdrawal from Gaza in August and September 2005. But the ongoing existence of the settlements continues to be a primary sore point with the Palestinians, who consider their ever-increasing isolation to be resulting in a form of apartheid.

Legend:
- Jewish outposts
- Jewish settlements
- Road and/or infrastructure line
- Areas controlled by settlements
- The "green line"

Bet Shean

Hadera

Mediterranean Sea

Netanya

Tel Aviv

Jordan River

Modi'in

Jericho

Ashdod

Jerusalem

Dead Sea

Beer Sheva

'Arad

Map 5: The Settlement Map

THE OSLO DECLARATION OF PRINCIPLES

The desire for a resolution of the conflict grew steadily during the late eighties. Many Israelis recognized that the continued occupation of Gaza and the West Bank could only lead to greater injustice to the Palestinians. Then, in 1990 Iraq invaded Kuwait and fired Scud missiles into Israel and Saudi Arabia. The United States with a number of allies responded and quickly defeated Saddam Hussein's forces. This victory created an opportunity for renewed efforts at regional peace.

Under the sponsorship of George H. W. Bush of the United States and Mikhail Gorbachev of the former Soviet Union, peace talks began in the fall of 1991 in Madrid. Palestinian and Israeli leaders, as well as representatives from Lebanon, Jordan, and Syria, attended. This meeting initiated ongoing negotiations aimed at establishing the framework for a lasting peace and for economic development in the region. This process was further stimulated by the election of Yitzhak Rabin of the Labor Party as Prime Minister of Israel.

The election of the Labor Party and the intifada were not the only sources of pressure for peace. Russia, the largest and most powerful country to emerge from the collapse of the former Soviet Union, encouraged the peace talks. The demise of the Soviet superpower, which had supported some Arab nations militarily for decades, and Russia's change of policy continues to play a role in resolving the Middle East conflicts. American politics also certainly contributed to hopes for peace in 1993. PLO officials said they moved toward an agreement with Israel because they believed President Bill Clinton's government was more pro-Israeli than any administration in the last quarter century.

In Norway, early in 1993, after several months of secret meetings, a plan that was called the Oslo Declaration of Principles was revealed. The effort to end the years of conflict culminated publicly in Washington, DC, in the presence of President Bill Clinton and a group of other supporters, on September 13, 1993. After the signing of an accord of mutual recognition and an outline for advancing peace negotiations, Arafat and Rabin shook hands.

A number of important outcomes can be noted. The assignment of authority in Gaza and the West Bank to the Palestinian National Authority (PNA) was made in May 1994. A peace treaty between Israel and Jordan was signed in October 1994. In September 1995 the first phase of the projected negotiations culminated in the signing of the Israeli-Palestinian Interim Agreement on the West Bank and the Gaza Strip, which broadened the means of Palestinian self-government. Still left unresolved, however, were such important issues as the possibility of the return of Palestinian refugees, the definition of the borders, and particularly the status of Jerusalem.

REACTIONS IN ISRAEL

A great deal had occurred in a relatively short time. There was open debate throughout Israel. Many Israelis were sympathetic to the Palestinians and wanted the conflict to end for personal as well as moral reasons. Many more, however, insisted that the security of Israel was most important and had to be guaranteed. Many Israelis, particularly the settlers, had demonstrated against the adoption of the Israeli-PLO accord.

On Saturday, November 4, 1995, after the conclusion of the Sabbath, a disgruntled right-wing Jewish radical named Yigal Amir turned the debate in a tragic direction. As Prime Minister Rabin was leaving a major peace rally in Tel Aviv, Amir attacked and killed Rabin. After the shock of this terrible deed began to subside, Shimon Peres, Rabin's successor as leader of the Labor Party, called for new elections. Much to everyone's surprise, Peres narrowly lost the election in May 1996 to Binyamin Netanyahu, leader of the right-of-center Likud Party. The primary reason given was the sense of insecurity that had been brought on by a series of suicide bombings and Netanyahu's strong insistence on making security the major issue in the election.

THE RISE OF HAMAS

The organization Hamas claimed responsibility for the bombings. Hamas (an Arabic acronym for "the Islamic Resistance Movement," or *Harakat al-Muqawamah al-Islamiyya*) evolved from the Muslim Brotherhood formed in the 1920s in Egypt. In 1978 the immediate predecessor of Hamas was formally registered in Israel under the name al-Mujamma al-Islami, an organization devoted primarily to providing social services. During the 1980s the character of the organization changed to one of active resistance against Israeli occupation, as reflected in the new name, Hamas.

The strength of Hamas was and is centered in the Gaza Strip. The area is the home of over a million people, most of whom live a very marginal existence. What there is presently in terms of health, welfare, and educational services is made possible largely by Hamas. The Palestine Liberation Organization had earlier administered a similar program. In 1988 Hamas published the Islamic Covenant, which set out its basic policy over against Israel and challenged the leadership of the PLO.

In the early 1990s the dominance of Hamas was strengthened significantly with the formation of the Izz al-Din al-Qassam Battalions. In the early stages the main targets of these militants were other Palestinians suspected of cooperating with the Israelis. Many suspected collaborators were assassinated. In time the strategy was expanded and attacks were mounted against Israeli military personnel and then Israeli civilians as well. Ambush, and particularly suicide bombings, became regular occurrences sponsored by Hamas. While Hamas was not solely responsible for Israel's unilateral withdrawal from Gaza in 2005 by any measure, in the eyes of the average Palestinian the stature of Hamas certainly increased.

During the 2000s Hamas has not withdrawn its intention to see Israel destroyed. Nor has it given up on militant efforts in support of that goal. But it has taken new initiative in the political sphere. It has gained wide acceptance in many parts of the West Bank beyond Gaza. These efforts enabled Hamas candidates to win the general election in 2006, and effectively to challenge the Palestinian Authority (the successor of the PLO) as the representative of the Palestinians. Neither Israel nor the United States had anticipated this happening. Whether either Israel or the United States will recognize Hamas and negotiate with the elected government is still uncertain. Both consider Hamas a terrorist organization and have demanded that Hamas disavow its repeated rejection of the right of Israel to exist as a free and secure nation. That has not happened thus far.

CONTINUING EFFORTS FOR PEACE

But back to the unfolding search for peace. After Netanyahu's election in 1996, efforts were made to continue on with the Oslo Accords. In 1997 Netanyahu joined with the Palestinian Authority in signing the Hebron Protocol. This agreement resulted in the turnover of much of the civilian administration of Hebron to the Palestinian Authority, but it also authorized the establishment of an Israeli settlement there. In 1998 the Wye River Conference in Maryland produced the Wye Agreement, which committed both the Palestinians and the Israelis to continued efforts to provide security for Israel and self-rule for Palestinians.

Early in 2000 President Clinton hosted Israeli Prime Minister Ehud Barak and Palestinian Chairman Yassir Arafat for a meeting at Camp David with the hope of reaching some agreement concerning outstanding issues such as the status of Jerusalem and the definition of borders. But no agreement was reached. Nonetheless, in June 2000 Israel unilaterally withdrew the remainder of its military from Lebanon, ending the eighteen-year occupation that had begun in 1982. The Islamic resistance group Hezbollah claimed some responsibility for this outcome.

THE AL-AQSA INTIFADA

On September 28, 2000, Ariel Sharon, leader of the Likud Party, accompanied a group of Israelis in what had become for them an annual visit to the Temple Mount (Haram al-Sharif to the Palestinians) to declare their right to exercise authority there. Though Sharon was not yet prime minister (that would take place in the 2001 Israeli election), he was a very public figure, well known for his hard-line approach concerning the aspirations of the Palestinians. Sharon had led the Israeli attack on Lebanon in 1982 and was a strong advocate for the establishment of Israeli settlements with the intention of laying practical and then real claim to the whole of the Occupied Territories for Israel. For Sharon to participate in the demonstration on Haram al-Sharif before two of the holiest of Muslim sites, the Al-Aqsa Mosque and the Dome of the Rock, outraged the Palestinians. On the day following Sharon's visit, Palestinians gathered at the Al-Aqsa Mosque in protest. Things turned ugly and Israeli soldiers fired on the demonstrators, killing five and injuring some two hundred. A new intifada began.

Whether Sharon's visit was the actual cause of the Second Intifada, also known as the Al-Aqsa Intifada, or just provided the justification for hostilities already planned is debated. The outcome was a cycle of violence marked by attack and counterattack between Palestinians and Israelis. Ehud Barak, the Israeli prime minister at the outbreak of the Al-Aqsa Intifada, tried to put an end to the escalation of violence. He called for special elections in 2001, hoping that a victory for him would enhance his authority in the eyes of the Palestinian leadership. But, as when Netanyahu had defeated Peres on the security issue, Ariel Sharon defeated Ehud Barak on the same issue. Israelis apparently believed that a tougher stance, with more use of power, was the right response to the intifada, and they voted accordingly.

Suicide bombings became an accepted mode of attack by the Palestinian resistance. In turn the Israeli military occupation became harsher. In 2002 Yassir Arafat was placed under house arrest in his headquarters in Ramallah. He remained there until he was taken to Paris for medical attention in November 2004. Arafat died in Paris on November 11, 2004, bringing to an end his long role as leader of the Palestinians.

Many areas of the West Bank that had been vacated by the Israeli army were again occupied and placed under military rule. Israel also began the construction of what they call a security fence. This barrier is constructed mainly along the borders between Israel and Jordan that were in place before the 1967 war, the so-called green line. However, in some instances— Palestinians would say many instances—the barrier claims new territory for Israel or separates Palestinian villages from their agricultural and grazing lands, as shown in map 6, "Israeli Wall/Fence." Further, this "fence" is in some places a formidable solid wall twenty feet tall. In 2004 the International Court of Justice ruled that the barrier violated international law. Subsequently the Israeli Supreme Court directed the government to make some changes in the placement of the barrier to enable the Arab population greater freedom of movement.

Thus far the construction of the barrier has continued. Many Israelis favor the barrier and defend it by citing the reduction in the number of suicide bombings and sniper shootings of Israelis by Palestinians. Those Israelis against it, and there are a number in that camp, urge a completely different approach to learning to live with their Palestinian neighbors, one based on justice. How the conflict will end is, obviously, not clear. By the end of 2005, as a result of the intifada, nearly one thousand Israelis and well over three thousand Palestinians had died, and most of the fatalities were civilian.

A STRATEGY OF DISENGAGEMENT

During the course of the intifada international powers made several efforts to try to halt the violence. In 2002 Crown Prince Abdullah of Saudi Arabia proposed a peace plan that was endorsed by the Arab League. In addition, the U.N. Security

Map 6: Israeli Wall/Fence

Council affirmed the desirability of a two-state solution to the conflict, a vision affirmed separately by President George W. Bush. In 2003 President Bush in concert with leaders of the United Nations, Russia, and the European Union issued the Road Map to Peace. In addition, that year a group of Palestinians and Israelis acting as individuals, not as representatives of their governments, put forward the Geneva Initiative. All of these efforts in one way or another urge the establishment of two independent and secure nations, one Palestinian and the other Israeli. Thus far, none of the initiatives has borne fruit.

Late in 2003 Ariel Sharon made a surprising announcement. As one response to the intifada he declared that Israel was willing to withdraw unilaterally from parts of the Occupied Territories. In June of 2004 Sharon gained the support of the Israeli government. In August 2004 Sharon set his plan in motion. Some Israeli citizens were forcibly evacuated from Gaza and the Israeli settlements there were demolished. The project was completed in September 2004.

Sharon also announced his intention of closing some of the smaller settlements scattered across the West Bank. He had become convinced that peace could not be established by negotiation or preserved so long as Israelis were intermingled with Palestinians in the Occupied Territories. The only realistically viable solution that Sharon could see was a total withdrawal from Gaza and a significant reduction of other Israeli settlements along with the construction of the security barrier. The Likud Party was not enthusiastic about Sharon's plan, so he quit Likud and formed a new party, Kadima. Disengagement—separation—became the policy he began to put into place.

The fruition of Sharon's plan was put into serious question early in 2006 when Sharon suffered a massive stroke, rendering him incapable of further governmental service. Ehud Olmert, who had been named as "acting" prime minister, won election as prime minister in April 2006 when the Kadima party won the most seats in the general election. Olmert is trying to pursue the same objectives set forth by Sharon, but it is not at all clear whether he has enough support from Israeli citizens.

A SECOND INVASION OF LEBANON

In early August 2006 what began as a very limited incursion into Israeli territory in the Galilee by members of Hezbollah turned into something much greater. Across the years since Israel's withdrawal from Lebanon, sporadic skirmishes had taken place. Members of Hezbollah occasionally fired rockets at Israeli military and civilian targets. Israelis fired back and sometimes launched air strikes against suspected Hezbollah sites near the border between Lebanon and Israel. The incident that set off the second invasion was the killing of eight Israeli soldiers and the abduction of two others. The Hezbollah leadership thought it might be able to negotiate the release of a number of Palestinian prisoners in a trade for the Israelis taken hostage.

Instead, Israel launched a major attack on Lebanon with the announced intention of wiping out Hezbollah once and for all. Air attacks were mounted against sites in southern Lebanon where Hezbollah was known to have strength. Further, the wider infrastructure (highways, bridges, airports) was demolished to try to slow if not prevent new supplies of military weapons being sent from Syria and Iran from reaching the Hezbollah troops. As part of this attack, large sections of the capital, Beirut, were also leveled. At the end of August, a ceasefire was brokered by the United Nations and other interested parties, and Israel withdrew from Lebanon, after enormous damage to property and the loss of many lives. As was the case with Hamas during the intifada in the 1990s, Hezbollah, in the aftermath of this conflict, may have emerged even stronger and more popular with Muslims, within and beyond Lebanon, than before it began. Public opinion, however, is mixed on this, and many, including Hassan Nasrallah, the leader of Hezbollah, acknowledge that the incursion of Hezbollah into Israel was a miscalculation that brought great destruction to Lebanon.

AN UNCERTAIN FUTURE

Most observers, of course, hope for a political solution. But the issues are complicated and difficult. What will be the fallout of Israel's extremely forceful retaliation against Hezbollah in Lebanon in 2006, internationally and internally? What will be the outcome of Hamas's violent removal of Fatah leadership in Gaza in June 2007? Will Hamas in Gaza and Fatah in the West Bank, each or either, be able to constitute governments with which Israel and the United States will agree to work? Has public opinion within Israel moved too far away from any realistic expectation for a secure peace for reconciliation to be possible? Will the Palestinian leadership give up an ideology of "all or nothing" and sincerely work for the establishment of a peaceful relationship with Israel in the pattern of Egypt and Jordan? With so many questions, it is no wonder that the future remains unclear.

This review of history has made clear one thing: conflict is not new to the land of Canaan, the land of Israel. As Eric Cline puts it:

There have been at least 118 separate conflicts in and for Jerusalem during the past four millennia—conflicts that ranged from local religious struggles to strategic military campaigns and that embraced everything in between. Jerusalem has been destroyed completely at least twice, besieged twenty-three times, attacked an additional fifty-two times, and captured and recaptured forty-four times. It has been the scene of twenty revolts and innumerable riots, has had at least five separate periods of violent terrorist attacks during the past century, and has only changed hands completely peacefully twice in the past four thousand years." (*Jerusalem Besieged,* p. 2)

For all who are directly and indirectly concerned about a just solution for both the Israelis and the Palestinians it is worth noting that the judgments that will be made and the actions that will be initiated will be based, at least in part, on theological perspective. The theology may be implicit or explicit, uninformed or intentional, denied or openly articulated, but some measure of theological opinion will be at work.

For Christians, the Bible provides another major source by which historical action is informed. While always fashioning judgment on the basis of history's realities, Christians also listen carefully to the Bible for its challenge to our prejudices and its declaration of God's values and agenda. Therefore, a review of biblical teaching concerning land is next.

QUESTIONS FOR DISCUSSION

1. In what ways have you experienced the accuracy of the author's contention that "theological reflection apart from historical reality can foster grave misunderstanding if not outright error." How do prejudice and religious fanaticism distort our understanding?

2. In the historical review, what came as new information? How is this interpretation of the "facts" different or similar to views you have previously encountered? How would you enhance or correct the author's review?

3. How would you characterize information you receive through the news media concerning Israel? Concerning the Arab nations? Is it fair? Balanced? How are Jews and Muslims sometimes stereotyped? Why are multiple witnesses or sources of information important, and how can you find them?

4. What are some of the insights gained in your reading that might lead to a reassessment of the conflict over land in Israel? How can theology or religious perspective influence the reading of history and political decision making?

FOR FURTHER READING

Armstrong, Karen. *Jerusalem: One City, Three Faiths*. New York: Ballantine Books, 1997.

Carter, Jimmy. *Palestine: Peace Not Apartheid*. New York: Simon and Schuster, 2006.

Cline, Eric H. *Jerusalem Besieged: From Ancient Canaan to Modern Israel*. Ann Arbor: University of Michigan Press, 2004.

Collins, Larry, and Dominique Lapierre. *0 Jerusalem!* New York: Simon & Schuster, 1972.

Friedman, Thomas L. *From Beirut to Jerusalem*. New York: Farrar, Straus & Giroux, 1989.

Johnson, Paul. *A History of the Jews*. New York: Harper/Collins, 1988.

Rodgers, Peter. *Herzl's Nightmare: One Land, Two Peoples*. New York: Nation Books, 2005.

Rudin, A. James. *Israel for Christians*. Philadelphia: Fortress Press, 1983.

Yapp, M. E. *The Near East since the First World War*. White Plains, NY: Longman, 1990.

3
God and Earth Keeping
Biblical Perspectives on Land

The Bible has much to say concerning land: from accounts of God's creation of all the land to disturbing examples of individuals and groups moving in and taking land by force from others. The Bible reports land promises, land gifts, land grabs, land crimes, land losses. In the Bible God is clearly related both to the land and to the people who reside in the land. God's involvement discloses a divine commitment to providing land while expecting justice, deliverance while expecting righteousness. In the Bible God creates a good world and intends all mortals to live in it responsibly and peaceably.

This chapter explores some of the many texts that address issues involving land. The aim is to gain some perspective on what is at stake from the Bible's viewpoint when we speak of the promised land, the land of Israel, land rights, the Holy Land, and God's land. Why indeed should we think about the Bible at all in connection with the modern, geopolitical entity Israel? Is the Bible at all relevant or instructive? That is the issue this chapter intends to explore.

THE BIBLE AND ETHICAL JUDGMENT

Let's begin with the last issue. Why should we consider the Bible when we struggle with such modern issues as territorial disputes between nations or among ethnic groups within a nation? What are we to make of the disastrous civil war that erupted in the former Yugoslavia, which featured the ethnic cleansing of Muslims by Christians? Or what should be the response of those who cherish the Bible to the conflicts so obvious between the Kurds, the Sunnis, and the Shiites in Iraq? And what about water rights, military occupation, civil disorder, and the multitude of concerns with which the real, live people in Israel must deal? How can the Bible help or hinder such a consideration? Does the Bible, in fact, provide single, clear-cut answers to such complex issues?

In shaping a response to questions such as these, it is important to recognize our limits. The Bible was not written with contemporary Israel (or any other part of today's geopolitical world) as its focus. It was written thousands of years ago in a much different historical and social setting. In that respect, the Bible is dated, an antiquity that may be interesting but little else. The Bible is not a legally binding land grant nor does it provide a blueprint for a predetermined future waiting irresistibly to unfold.

Nonetheless, the Bible is a book treasured, cherished, read, and reread by three significant faith communities in our modern world. For Jews, the Bible comprises the books that Protestants call the Old Testament. For Christians, the Bible obviously includes the New Testament as well. For Catholic and Orthodox Christians, the Bible also contains material in the Old Testament called the Apocrypha, which neither Jews nor Protestants acknowledge as part of the Bible. Muslims also honor the books of the Old and New Testaments, though they claim that significant alterations should be made to understand these books properly. Despite differences that clearly exist between Jews, Christians, and Muslims with respect to the whole collection of materials that is generally called the Bible, it is true that each faith community holds the Bible in special regard and honors it as God's word.

It is also important to recognize that all three groups also cherish and employ materials not included in the Bible in fashioning their theological and ethical positions on questions such as land rights and land responsibilities. Christians have assembled a vast assortment of literature that aims at interpreting and institutionalizing the teachings of the Bible. From the earliest beginnings of the Christian movement until the present, Christians have collected and pondered the writings of persons recognized as spiritually mature. Jews utilize the ongoing interpretation of the Bible in the Oral Law found in books such as the Talmud, which continues down to the present day. Indeed, Judaism is not dependent primarily upon the Bible for its views concerning land but upon the continuing commentary and reflection through the generations that provides rich ethical and religious instruction. Muslims rely primarily upon the Koran, which includes many biblical traditions but is much more. Further, there is a vast literature that reflects upon the implications of the Koran for life in community.

The task of interpreting the Bible and other important traditions is not a simple one. For some, the "Word of God" is equated with the biblical "words." For others, God's Word is heard as the faith community responds by interpreting and obeying the ancient Word in contemporary settings. The Bible seldom if ever can be applied directly and literally to answer concrete, complex legal and ethical questions, but it does provide guidelines and direction; it suggests the right questions to ask as people of faith struggle to be faithful.

For people active in faith communities, the issue is not *whether* to consider the Bible when dealing with the tough questions of life, but *how*. The approach taken in this volume is to consider the Bible carefully with the intent of gaining understanding. The task is not to determine which view is correct, oldest, or most authoritative. Rather, the goal is to listen and reflect upon the events that God's people have experienced and the reports they have passed along in the hope and with the conviction that God continues to care for and give guidance to those who seek to place God's agenda foremost in their lives.

It is important to note at the outset that the theme of human responsibility before God is a primary motif found throughout the biblical accounts. Much less is said about land rights than about the allegiance owed to God by all human beings, by those whom God has set as earth keepers in the midst of creation. Responsible, just action within God's land and care for the land become the guiding norms. Such responsibility must be brought to reality in the real, historical world of politics and power, and thus the success or failure of every attempt at dominion can be measured against the Bible's call for righteousness, for love, for mercy, for justice, for the God-fearing exercise of the full range of responsibilities that God has given to human earth keepers appointed for this purpose.

THE PROMISED LAND

The promise of land is one of the basic themes found first in Genesis and echoed in other parts of the Bible. Abram and Sarai at God's command leave the country of their families on a quest for "the land that I will show you" (Gen. 12:1). With the promise of becoming a great nation, becoming famous, and providing a blessing for many, the forebears of the people of Israel (and the other Abrahamic peoples, for that matter) set out from southern Mesopotamia eventually to find their way to the land of Canaan, which would much later (in the time of the Romans) be called Palestine (Gen. 12:4–6). When they reached "the land," God appeared to Abram and gave a promise that was to encourage and guide countless people for centuries to come: "To your offspring I will give this land" (Gen. 12:7).

The narrative concerning Abram and Sarai is well known and is built around the promise of posterity and land given by God. There are threats to Abram and Sarai (Gen. 12:17–20;

13:8–18; 14:13–16; 20:8–18). Covenants are made (Gen. 15:17–21; 17:1–14) and new names, Abraham and Sarah (Gen. 17:5, 15), are given, but the promises of land and posterity are repeated at each new step on the way (Gen. 12:7; 13:14–17; 15:5, 7, 18–21; 17:4–8). The drama reaches its climax when Isaac, the long-awaited though not really expected heir of Abraham and Sarah (15:2–4; 16:1–4; 17:16–21; 18:9–15; 21:1–7), is designated as the offering that God wants Abraham to make as a sign of his allegiance (Gen. 22:1–2). Abraham sets out to do God's bidding, but at the last moment, is stopped from carrying out the horrible deed and is once again given the divine assurance of posterity and land (Gen. 22:9–18).

In the all-too-human stories of the descendants of Abraham and Sarah, each new generation is again met by God and given promises of children and land: first Isaac (Gen. 26:3–4) and then Jacob (Gen. 28:3–4, 13–15; 35:9–12). The promise is remembered at the death of Jacob (Gen. 48:21), and again when Joseph's days are over (Gen. 50:24). Centuries later, when God encounters Moses at a burning bush, the divine self-identification includes a reference to those to whom the promise had been made generations earlier (Exod. 3:6, 15). The offspring of Abraham and Sarah, though enslaved in Egypt, were not forgotten. God sent Moses to lead them out and to guide them to the land promised first to Abraham and Sarah, the land of the Canaanites (Exod. 3:8, 15–17; 6:3–8). The theme of "promised land" continues until it is fulfilled in the book of Joshua with Israel's entry into Canaan (Josh. 24:1–13).

The promise to Abraham and Sarah was remembered long after its initial fulfillment. It was included in the rendition of God's faithfulness in Psalm 105 and in Ezra's recital before the people after the return from exile (Neh. 9:7). God's faithfulness to the promise at the time of Jesus' birth is noted in Luke 1:55, 73. That the promise included blessing that would flow through Abraham to all peoples (Gen. 12:3; 22:18; 26:4; 28:14) was remembered as well (Isa. 19:24; Zech. 8:13; Acts 3:25; Gal. 3:8–9).

In the traditions concerning "promised land," it's essential to recognize the this-world character of the divine commitment. While the fulfillment of the promise that led Abram and Sarai out of Mesopotamia lay in the future, the land they were to seek was real land, territory in this world, not just a metaphorical place. Across the centuries, Jews interpreted the promise of land in many ways, but as is seen in the deep, ongoing love for Jerusalem especially, for most Jews the real, this-world character of the promise has continued to have special significance. Jerusalem was not only a symbol; it was a real place where people could live and work and worship. God's promise represented an intention, as the Jews understood it, that they would have a real place in this world where they could live out their lives fully as God's people. The land promise became central to Jewish identity.

For many Christians, either the promise of land was spiritualized—understood as a reference to a spiritual reality, such as heaven—or it was ignored altogether. For many Western Christians, the notion of a special, God-promised land was seen as an unworthy relic of a narrow, particularistic religion (meaning Judaism), which they believed had rightly been recognized as nonessential by the more enlightened universalism of Christianity. The Eastern church, however, continued to celebrate the special place of Jerusalem and Palestine, though in ways that all too often ignored or disdained Jewish understandings of the biblical tradition. Nevertheless, the material, this-worldly aspect of God's gifts was maintained and honored. The spiritual and the worldly met at particular times in real places, and that is of significance.

For Muslims Jerusalem took on special importance because, according to tradition, Jerusalem was Muhammad's destination in his night visit from Mecca. But further, the land of Palestine became important because for centuries it has been the home for generations of Muslims. They have not so much considered Palestine as "promised" to them but as theirs by right of habitation. The same can be said of many Christian Arabs who have also long lived in Palestine.

THE LAND OF ISRAEL

From the beginning of recorded history, people have lived along the eastern coastline of the Mediterranean Sea. For several thousand years before Abraham and Sarah—who in turn lived at least five hundred years before the emergence of the biblical people called Israel—people worked the land, raised flocks, developed various trades, fought with one another occasionally, and did all the other things that mark human societies. These were not modern people, to be sure, but they were not primitive, either. They left written records of their culture, in some instances, and numerous artifacts attesting to their presence in the land.

By the time the Bible was taking shape, these people had come to be called Canaanites (Gen. 10:19; 24:3; Deut. 1:7; 11:30; Neh. 9:24), or in a more specific manner the population was said to include "the Kenites, the Kenizzites, the Kadmonites, the Hittites, the Perizzites, the Rephaim, the Amorites, the Canaanites, the Girgashites, and the Jebusites" (Gen. 15:19–21). The "land of Canaan" was a common term of reference.

Into the land of Canaan, the territory occupied by men, women, and children referred to as Canaanites, came the people of Israel. The historical evidence is not conclusive about precisely when or how Israel moved in. The biblical narrative in some places suggests that Israel's occupation resulted from a decisive series of battles under the leadership of Joshua (Josh. 6; 8; 10–11). Other biblical passages, however, make clear that the process was not as unambiguous as it first appears (Josh. 13:1–7, 13; 16:10; 17:12; Judg. 1:27–33). Further, they had competition for the land from the Philistines, who moved in on the coast after failing in their attempt to enter Egypt. From the biblical witness and archaeological work, we know that one group of people, generally termed Canaanites, was displaced or brought under domination of another group, the Israelites, across a time span of approximately two hundred years. Sudden battles, gradual encroachment, treaties, intermarriage with Canaanites, trade—all of these seem to have played a part. But the end result is clear: the land of Canaan eventually became the land of Israel.

The process culminated with the crowning of David, son of Jesse, as king (2 Sam. 5:1–5). For some two hundred years, the people had been loosely associated as clans that occasionally acted in concert, usually for defense (Judg. 5). Saul, a Benjaminite, was chosen as the first king of Israel (1 Sam. 8–12; but consider Abimelech in Judg. 9), but he had only moderate success in bringing the people together. Under David a unified government was instituted. David, first recognized as king by Judah (2 Sam. 2:1–4), created a government that utilized clan or tribal allegiance but went beyond it. Jerusalem, a Jebusite or Canaanite city belonging to none of the tribes, was captured and made the capital (2 Sam. 5:6–10). The ark, the symbol of God's presence, was brought to Jerusalem as a sign of the new unity (2 Sam. 6). David consolidated his borders (2 Sam. 8–10) and thus began what we call the "united kingdom," which lasted approximately eighty years. In the united kingdom the northern and southern tribes were ruled effectively by one king—first David and then his son Solomon.

During the united monarchy, the kingdom reached its maximum size. The phrase "from Dan to Beersheba" expressed the extent of Israel's territory (Judg. 20:1; 1 Sam. 3:20; 2 Sam. 24:2, 6, 15), indicating the far north to the far south. David is remembered as extending his rule to the east of the Jordan River over Edom, Moab, Ammon, and part of Syria, while also bringing the Philistines on the coastal plain under his control (2 Sam. 8, 10). Solomon maintained David's conquests and pushed the border southward to the Gulf of Eilat (or Aqaba), which leads into the Red Sea. The Negev or southern desert became part of the kingdom. Thus, at its largest, Israel extended from Eilat in the south almost to Mount Hermon in the north, and from the Mediterranean on the west to the Jordan River on the east. Further, Israel effectively exercised political control over some parts of the nations east of the Jordan.

The question of borders is important. Some modern Jews and Christians contend that modern Israel has a right to the territory claimed at the time of Solomon's kingdom. The biblical sources are difficult to interpret, however, and leave questions (Exod. 23:31; Num. 34:1–12). How far north did the kingdom extend? Where exactly was Dan (Josh. 19:40–48; 1 Kgs. 5:1–12; 9:10–14; 2 Sam. 24:5–7)? How much of the southern desert was controlled (Josh. 15:1–63; 1 Kgs. 9:26)? What about the coastal plain, particularly the Philistine cities (1 Kgs. 2:36–46)? And how long were the nations east of the Jordan kept subservient (1 Kgs. 11:5–7, 14–25)? Even if the exact borders could be determined, it is not at all clear that Solomon's borders should become the geographic definition of the "promised land." Nor does it automatically follow that land promised, received, and lost two thousand years ago is rightly claimed again on the basis of biblical warrant. The question of borders entails all these questions and more, and we shall need to consider some of these more fully later.

The kingdom built by David and expanded by Solomon was relatively short-lived. When Solomon died, his son Rehoboam was unable to sustain the union between north and south. The northern tribes rejected Rehoboam and selected Jeroboam (1 Kgs. 12), while Judah and Benjamin remained loyal to Rehoboam. Thus began a period that saw two kingdoms, Israel in the north and Judah in the south. This situation lasted until Israel was destroyed by the Assyrians in 721 BCE and became an Assyrian province. The southern kingdom, Judah, came to an end when the Babylonians destroyed Jerusalem and the temple of Solomon in 587 BCE. Persia subsequently took control of the former territories of Israel and Judah in 539 BCE. Alexander the Great's empire continued the domination of what had been Israel's land during the fourth century and into the second century BCE. The Maccabean Revolt returned independence to Jews in and around Jerusalem for a period of about 130 years (166–37 BCE) before Roman power once again brought an end to Judean autonomy. Not until 1948 CE did Jews again experience any political authority over land in Palestine.

This brief historical review is intended to demonstrate three things. First, when Israel took possession of the land it believed it had been promised, it did so by displacing those already there. Laying claim to territory necessitated conflict, and keeping territory likewise required force. It was not as if Israel had taken unclaimed land. Quite the contrary, Israel took occupied, settled, titled land, the land of someone else.

Second, only for a brief eighty years did a unified Israel actually rule the "promised land." During most of the time before and after David and Solomon, the forebears of the Jews shared the land with other people in a variety of political arrangements with varying degrees of autonomy for the Israelites.

Third, the real or ideal specifications of the land of Israel are difficult to determine because, in the Bible, the boundaries were vaguely defined. Thus, even if they were a basis for modern claims, the exact boundaries of the domain of David and Solomon are unclear.

LAND RIGHTS AND RESPONSIBILITIES

The issue of land rights is central to many who live in or are concerned about the Middle East and especially modern Israel. Who has a "right" to be there? How shall land rights be determined? When do the interests and needs of a community supersede individual claims? What shall be done to compensate for land taken as a result of war? Who will determine fairness, justice? How long should these concerns remain unsettled?

In most instances, the Bible does not answer these questions directly. It offers a framework, however, that assists those who wish or are constrained to deal with land issues. The biblical perspective is disturbing to many because it places emphasis on land responsibilities rather than land rights. What is done in and with the land and how it is done are the primary concerns, though I will say more about land rights later. Nonetheless, insight can be gained from the biblical traditions bearing on the matters at hand.

Let's begin with how Israel came to occupy the land of Canaan. We have already considered how Israel, over the course of several hundred years, acquired the land through a combina-

tion of military victories, treaties, purchases, gradual encroachment and settlement, and default on the part of prior occupants.
Between approximately 1200 BCE and 950 BCE the Israelites
became the dominant political group in Palestine. In terms of
population size and economic power, they probably exceeded
other groups still in the land.

Certainly these accomplishments warranted a literary epic,
but if such an epic ever existed, it has been lost. What we do
have in the Bible is an account with a much different tone and
purpose. Specific stories celebrate victories or emphasize Israel's
accomplishments, but overall the biblical story stresses Israel's
responsibility in the land, a responsibility to God, to kin, and
to other human beings.

The Bible emphasizes that Israel was *given* the land. Deuteronomy makes this especially clear. Certainly the promise of land
is explicit (Deut. 6:23; 7:8; 8:1), but the emphasis is on the
utter graciousness of the divine act: The people were without
merit (Deut. 7:7; 9:5–6). God brought the people out of Egypt
and into a rich land (Deut. 6:10–11; 7:19; 8:7–10). The Lord
cared for the people through the wilderness wanderings despite
their stubborn rebelliousness (Deut. 8:15–16; 9:6–14). The
land was given to Israel because of God's generous care.

A corollary to God's giving the land to Israel is God's
expelling of the prior occupants. According to the Bible it is
God, not Israel, who is responsible for removing the Canaanites
(Deut. 7:1, 17–21; 8:17–18; Josh. 23:5). While reports of military victory are preserved—where Joshua, for instance, can be
said to have taken the land or defeated his enemies (Josh. 11:23;
12:7)—the emphasis remains on God giving the land (Josh.
1:2; 2:9, 24; 8:1). Further, the dispossessing of the Canaanites
was not an immoral, capricious act of God but a divine response
to their wicked behavior (Deut. 7:23–26; 9:4–5). According to
the account, God also warned the Israelites that if they dis-
obeyed the Almighty as had the Canaanites, they too would be
punished and perish from the land (Deut. 8:11–20).

Some, particularly Christians, find the traditions of Israel's
entry into Canaan brutal and inhumane; the total destruction

and execution of all survivors (Josh. 6:20–21) horrify these people. That the carnage resulted from what was understood to be God's command (Deut. 7:2, 16, 24) further offends them. Some Christians declare these texts to be typical of the Old Testament as a whole and reject them outright, contending that such a view of God is inferior—indeed inimical—to God as revealed in Jesus of Nazareth.

In response, several points should be noted. First, texts calling for the utter, complete destruction of an enemy are few, and thus it is not fair to contend that these texts are typical of the First Testament.

Second, the reason for the divine command was to keep Israel from being tempted to follow the idolatrous and wicked ways of those being destroyed (Deut. 6:13–15; 7:5–6; Lev. 18:24–25). Those being displaced were understood to be evil and deserving punishment. Thus, this is no wanton killing for killing's sake.

Third, the threat of destruction made and carried out against some of the Canaanites was also made against Israel as well. For anyone concerned, whether Canaanites or Israelites, disregarding God's way would bring destruction. Indeed, the belief that Jesus was executed in the place of sinners rightly deserving death and the conviction of a Last Judgment are in some ways in harmony with the idea of punishment found in some passages in Deuteronomy and Joshua.

And fourth, the mass destruction of the population of Canaan did not take place (Josh. 13:1–7, 13; 16:10; 17:12; Judg. 1:27–33; 3:5). Indeed, many Canaanites continued in the land. Archaeology confirms the ongoing presence of the Canaanites, as do a number of biblical accounts. Later generations of Israelites continually found the ways of their Canaanite neighbors appealing, and they often adopted them. This is in fact cited at the end of Judah's history as a primary reason for the divine judgment that fell on Judah (2 Kgs. 23:26–27; Jer. 2:4–37; 5:1–17; 44:1–30).

This leads us into the question of responsibility in relation to the occupation of the land as understood in the Bible. Deuteronomy sets forth the requirement that, to keep the land, the Israelites must obey God's commandments (Deut. 4:25–26; 30:15–20). Other passages make clear the same connection (Josh. 23:6–13; Lev. 18:2–5; 20:22–26; 26:27–33; 1 Kgs. 9:6–9; Ezek. 33:29).

The rules regulating life in the land were varied, extensive, and detailed. Within the books of Exodus, Leviticus, and Deuteronomy are numerous exhortations and proscriptions aimed at establishing a society pleasing to God. The rules governed ritual, lending and commerce, family matters, warfare, relations between rich and poor, treatment of captives and slaves, and many other aspects of life.

The codes are stated briefly in several places. For instance, there are the well-known Ten Commandments (Exod. 20:1–17; Deut. 5:1–21). The essence of these commandments can be stated as serving the one God loyally and humbly and working for justice and compassion within the human community (Deut. 10:12–22; Mic. 6:8). Jesus summed up the law and commandments in much this same way (Matt. 22:34–40; Mark 12:28–34; Luke 10:25–28). Living in accord with these ordinances was central to serving God and crucial to realizing the fullness of life intended by God.

From the biblical perspective, therefore, land rights are subordinate to land responsibilities. Israel displaced the former inhabitants of the land because the Canaanites had lived in ways inappropriate before God. Israel had no right to the land as such, though a promise had been given. The divine promise did not entitle Israel necessarily to Canaan, but rather called for obedient living in expectation that God would eventually provide a proper inheritance for God's people. For Israel, life in the land was explicitly contingent upon allegiance to God and the faithful, loving establishment of justice and peace within the community.

Many Christians believe, as do some Jews and most Muslims, that ancient Israel lost the land of Canaan because of disobedience before God. Certainly the prophets pronounced such a judgment, first on the northern kingdom (Amos 2:6–16; 9:7–10) and then on the southern kingdom as well (Jer. 5:20–6:30).

What's more, if that were not decisive enough, some believe that the destruction of Jerusalem in 70 CE was again divine punishment that brought the final expulsion of the Jews from Canaan and the end to all rightful claims (if any ever existed) on the land. Some use New Testament texts to support such contentions (Mark 13:1–13; John 12:37–50; 14:6; Acts 7:51–53; Gal. 3:6–4:7).

This reasoning has two problems. It assumes that (1) at one time Israel was faithful enough to warrant the land, and (2) the point of the Bible is to validate land claims. The Bible contains little if any support for either of these assumptions. As noted previously, Israel was reminded from the outset that it was not its worthiness that prompted God's gracious gift. Moreover, once Israel was in the land, the Bible offers account after account of Israel's disobedience. No attempt is made in the Bible, nor should it be made now, to claim a guarantee to land entitlement on the basis of God's grace.

The message of the passages about the land was that Israel was given stewardship of the land. Occupation and responsible action were inseparably bound. A place was graciously provided for Israel to develop a community that could show the world what God intended for humanity. God's aim was not to make a perpetual land grant but to offer a place for a society to emerge in which God's way was paramount. Land was granted for faithful living before God and with one another.

One other matter should be considered. Some Jews admit that autonomy over a special land may not be absolutely essential for faithful Jewish living. Nonetheless, it is only in a place of safety, where the social structure can be arranged to allow a rigorous pursuit of the ordinances, that the full possibilities can be realized. This does not mean that Jews must be allowed a land at the expense of others, but it helps to explain the special regard that most Jews hold for modern Israel. The full possibilities for justice can only be realized in a community that controls its own space. The full possibilities of faithfulness before God can only be demonstrated when it is truly possible to make choices and to set appropriate policies. For centuries Jews in liturgy and in practice have expressed such convictions.

From a biblical perspective, life before God always involves human community, and human community always involves specific space (that is, land) where community life can be ordered and experienced. Too many Christians, particularly in the West, disdain or disregard the significance of the reality that we are flesh. They become susceptible to an individualized, privatized, spiritualized form of Christianity that is quite alien to the biblical tradition, with its insistence upon land, incarnation, corporeality, and God's concern for the whole of creation, the world in all its concreteness. Thus, they ignore or misinterpret the importance of land for responsible living before God.

THE HOLY LAND

Some people interested in the religious significance of the land refer to Palestine as the Holy Land. Christians, especially, use the term "Holy Land" to refer to the places where Jesus was born and raised, where he ministered and was crucified and raised from the dead. Thus, for Christians the Holy Land theoretically means Palestine as a whole but actually centers on Bethlehem, Nazareth, a portion of the area around the Sea of Galilee, and Jerusalem. Most of the Christian holy sites are located in these places and are revered for their direct association with Jesus. The specific location of many of these shrines, however, is based only on tradition, dating back to Constantine the Great (fourth century CE). Many owe their identification to Constantine's mother, Queen Helena, who visited the area after she became a Christian.

Jews often use the term "Holy Land" as a reference to Israel. This term has been used frequently in Jewish writings from the second century CE to the present. In Jewish usage the term is broader than in Christian use and emphasizes places less significant for Christians: Hebron, Shechem, Jericho, Bethel,

Beersheba. Indeed, when Jews say Holy Land, they think of the whole of the land through which Abraham and Sarah traveled. Sometimes the term "Holy Land" is used in place of Israel, which can be understood as a political reference. Usually, though, the term is just another way—a more religious way—that Jews, like Christians, refer to the setting so special to them, the setting of so much of the tradition recounted in the Bible.

The Bible itself, however, virtually never uses the term "Holy Land." Only in one text, Zechariah 2:12, is the term explicitly employed when referring to Judah as *God's* special inheritance in "the holy land." Otherwise, the references to holy places in the Bible are predominantly to Jerusalem (Isa. 52:1; Neh. 11:1, 18) or Mount Zion, located within Jerusalem (Pss. 2:6; 3:4; 15:1; Joel 3:17). More specifically, the Temple (Ps. 5:7) and its innermost sanctuary (1 Kgs. 6:16; 8:6) were referred to as "holy." In the same manner, the tabernacle of the premonarchy period had its special holy place.

Things are considered holy when they are in close contact with God. God's name is holy, and God's Spirit is holy. The Sabbath is dedicated to God and is therefore holy (Exod. 20:8, 31:14). In God's presence ground may become holy (Exod. 3:5).

The people are holy because God has chosen them especially (Exod. 19:6), but their holiness comes from being set apart by God, not from their own character. In Leviticus, the people of Israel are enjoined to be holy because God is holy. And how are they to do so? By keeping God's commandments (Lev. 19:3–37; see 1 Pet. 1:15–16)! Detailed ordinances are given by which the people as a holy people are to live. It is in the midst of these instructions that the description of a very distinctive institution—the jubilee year—was placed. It is the culmination of the commandments by which this chosen people would demonstrate divine holiness.

The jubilee year is to occur every fifty years as a Sabbath for seven "weeks of years" (Lev. 25:8). The most distinctive feature of the jubilee year is that property originally received at the distribution of the land when Israel entered Canaan reverts to the extended family (clan or tribe) to which it was first given (Lev.

25:13). Thus, no family can fall into perpetual servitude. If property is lost as payment of debt, it is returned at the jubilee (Lev. 25:28, 31). Those who sell themselves or their children into slavery in payment of debts will be released (Lev. 25:41). The possession of land is the guarantee that all may live in a measure of freedom. The jubilee year was the administrative mechanism by which God's intentions could be realized.

The theological foundation for this unique institution is this: the land was never understood as belonging to Israel at all. It *belonged* to God! All humans are dependent upon God's graciousness and are allowed to use the land at God's pleasure. Thus, all are to have compassion for one another, to love and care for neighbors, to be holy as God is holy. God's land is only loaned to them, and every fifty years there is a radical reminder of this God-defined arrangement.

There is no clear evidence that the year of jubilee was actually observed. Jeremiah contains a record of something like it being tried, but major differences from the Levitical jubilee existed in the aborted effort (Jer. 34:1–22). Nonetheless, the ideal is clear. Because God owns the land, the people of Israel are never more than caretakers. They are not free to do whatever they wish in the land because, in the end, it is not theirs. At the same time, they are not less than caretakers, either, because the land is entrusted to them for safekeeping. They are to deal with one another justly. They are to act responsibly and strive to be the holy people they were chosen to be.

When we refer to Israel or Palestine as the Holy Land, we would do well to remember that the biblical perspective is much more concerned with the people in that land and their faithful stewardship of it than the land itself. The significance of all things "holy" is that they point to the source of all holiness: God, the Holy One of Israel. Apart from God nothing is holy. Christians during the Crusades did a terrible disservice to God and committed atrocity when they massacred countless "unbelievers," "infidels," in their misconceived effort to rescue the Holy Land. The land can be holy only if the people in it honor God's way. The Crusades were far from holy. Holiness does not reside in the land but in the God to whom the land belongs and before whom all are to seek to live justly, honorably, and compassionately.

GOD'S LAND

The modern nation of Israel, *Medinat Yisrael* in Hebrew, is situated in *Eretz Yisrael,* literally in Hebrew "the land of Israel." The word *eretz* can designate several things: from a specific territory such as "the land of your sojournings" (Gen. 28:4; Exod. 6:4) or "the land of the Philistines" (Gen. 21:32, 34; Exod. 13:17) to "earth" as parallel with "heaven" (Gen. 24:3). Sometimes *eretz* means "ground," as when something or someone falls to the ground (2 Sam. 2:22; 14:11; 2 Kgs. 10:10). Despite contemporary usage, *Eretz Yisrael,* in the sense of being the whole territory, occurs rather infrequently (1 Sam. 13:19; Ezek. 40:2; 47:18; 1 Chr. 22:2; 2 Chr. 2:17; 34:7). Another Hebrew word, *adamah,* also can be translated "land." But *adamah* generally means "dirt" (1 Sam. 4:12; Isa. 45:9), "cultivated land" as opposed to wilderness (Gen. 2:5; 47:23).

The multiple meanings of *eretz* lead to another insight: God not only owns the land, but God also creates the earth. By opening as it does with the creation story, the Bible presents an affirmation with far-reaching consequences. In the first chapter of Genesis, God alone creates the earth and then sets about to make it a good place for all living things. Humankind is created in God's very image (Gen. 1:26–27) and is given authority over and responsibility for keeping all the earth (Gen. 1:28–30). In the most fundamental way, then, the earth belongs to the God of Israel. And human beings? They are stewards, earth keepers, responsible to God, the earth's creator.

From a biblical perspective, any discussion of land finally must acknowledge divine ownership and dominion. Human land claims are always secondary, derived, conditional. Human owners and occupants come and go, but God remains; the land—indeed the whole earth—is God's. The only totally adequate way to refer to particular land and to the whole of the earth is to call it God's land.

Of course, in our modern world many scorn the notion that there is a God and even more that God has created and thereby rightly claims the earth as divine territory and domain. To take the biblical perspective, however, is to affirm this very idea. From this point of view, human responsibility is recognized as awesome, and human claims of ownership are never seen as absolute. Scripture is clear that God intends blessing. The inhabitants of earth become the agents and participants of God's stewardship of God's land as earth keepers. Activities and claims that run counter to this basic affirmation are thus suspect for those who wish to be guided by the Bible.

A NEW HEAVEN AND A NEW EARTH

Both Jewish and Christian traditions contain the hope for a new world, a new heaven and a new earth, which God will create to replace our existing earth with all of its pain and injustice. This visionary or eschatological (dealing with the end of the world) view is not dominant, but it is persistent and powerful. Within the Bible and in each generation subsequent to it, this vision was for some people the source of encouragement to endure, and was the basis for a hope that had little concrete reality in their own lives. What can we learn from this understanding of land?

The vision is rooted in the prophetic view of God's judgment and restoration of the people and the land. The imagery used by the prophets included the shaking of the heavens and the earth as God punished iniquity (Amos 9:5–6; Joel 3:16). Similarly, God's forgiveness will bring blessing on the land in the form of abundant crops and lush vegetation (Amos 9:13–15; Joel 3:18). Likewise, the human community will be made whole; injustice will be banished and injuries healed (Zeph. 3:14–20; Hos. 14:4–7; Isa. 25:6–8). A peaceful kingdom will be established, where God's way prevails (Isa. 11:1–9; 65:17–25).

This imagery is figurative rather than literal. The writers used poetic exaggeration aimed at expressing the seriousness of judgment and the grandeur of restoration. As the tradition developed, however, some understood the language in a more direct manner: a new heaven and a new earth would replace the worn-out, corrupted world of present experience (Isa. 66:22; 2 Pet. 3:10, 13; Rev. 21:1–4). This viewpoint, found relatively infrequently in the Bible, was elaborated extensively in literature outside the Bible. It is known as apocalypticism. Many mistakenly believe that the apocalyptic vision of the end of the world is primary in the Bible. It is not. A great deal of speculation and misinformation has been generated by this inaccurate appraisal of the Bible's teaching.

Nonetheless, whether one understands the imagery to be literal or not, it is important to recognize that a place, a land, is essential to the realization of God's ways. Punishment is described in terms of earthly experience: drought, pestilence, war, death. Restoration or forgiveness is expressed in equally concrete terms: rescue from danger, release of prisoners, healing of disease, peace, and abundant crops. The Bible seems not to recognize disembodied punishment or salvation. To those who wrote the Bible, it was simply inconceivable that there could be no place of God's choosing, no Jerusalem, no land. Radical renewal might be necessary—even the creation of a new heaven, a new earth, a new Jerusalem—but God's interaction with humanity could only be expressed in terms of concrete, material existence. We should hesitate to forsake this understanding too quickly, even though the imagery does not fit readily into our contemporary worldview. After all, it is not much stranger than the insistence among Christians that the presence of Jesus is known in the sharing of bread and the fruit of the vine.

CONCLUDING REFLECTION

The biblical perspectives we have explored are varied. The importance of land (earth) and the land (the land of Canaan) cannot be denied. God's promise of land and occupation of the land constitute a major theme in the narrative from Genesis through Joshua. The necessity of a space, a land, for the faithful following of God's ways—with accompanying blessing and punishment—is made clear in numerous passages. The insistence that it is God alone who can give land is based on the radical recognition that the land—all the land, the earth—finally belongs only to God. And God may even provide a new earth and a new heaven if need be so that human community and life may reach the fullness that God wills.

To disregard this rich and diverse tradition means ignoring or abandoning the Bible. For some who disregard the tradition of land, this leads to rejecting especially the Hebrew Scriptures, the Old Testament, as inadequate, inferior, or erroneous. Many Christians take this course and insist on a spiritual understanding that claims to be universal and free of such mundane issues as land. Unfortunately, historically speaking, these same Christians have all too often been concerned with seizing land, imposing their views, and governing over as many others as possible. The proper response to the concreteness of the Bible is neither a falsely literal biblicism nor an arrogantly disdainful modernism. Rather, those who seek to adopt the biblical perspective will listen carefully to the tradition, seeking to discern how it may instruct us amid the complex realities of our contemporary world. This may not always be easy, but it is critical and excitingly engaging. To this task we turn in the next chapter.

QUESTIONS FOR DISCUSSION

1. How is the Bible viewed by the author and considered important in thinking about current issues? What are the limitations of the Bible? In what ways do you agree or disagree with the author's point of view?
2. Which of the themes considered in this chapter was most familiar? Least familiar? What surprised you, came as new information, or intrigued you about the biblical material?

3. What are some of the ways the Old Testament and New Testament agree or disagree about the issue of land? What is gained by having both Testaments? How do they complement/supplement one another?
4. How pervasive is the divine requirement of human responsibility and how is it related to land? How are the themes of human responsibility and divine ownership of land connected? How is God's ownership of the land (and all the earth) expressed?

FOR FURTHER READING

Brueggemann, Walter. *The Land: Place as Gift, Promise, and Challenge in Biblical Faith*. Minneapolis: Fortress Press, 1977.

Davies, W. D. *The Gospel and the Land*. Berkeley: University of California Press, 1974.

Evans, Bernard F., and Gregory D. Cusack, eds. *Theology of the Land*. Collegeville, MN: Liturgical Press, 1987.

Habel, Norman C. *The Land Is Mine: Six Biblical Land Theologies*. Minneapolis: Augsburg Fortress, 1995.

Heschel, Abraham Joshua. *Israel: An Echo of Eternity*. New York: Farrar, Straus & Giroux, 1987.

Lilburne, Geoffrey R. *A Sense of Place: A Christian Theology of the Land*. Nashville: Abingdon Press, 1989.

Prior, Michael. *The Bible and Colonialism: A Moral Critique*. Sheffield, UK: Sheffield Academic Press, 1997.

4
God's Way and Israel
Theological Reflections on a Particular Land

For Christians, the activities of governments and societies are always subject to scrutiny and criticism. The starting point for any analysis is the conviction that God as creator and ruler has the final authority and is the ultimate judge. All human behavior is to be measured against God's way, God's norm. Such a theological assertion finds support within the Bible but is also based on creedal statements developed by the church. For Christians, theological tradition, as well as the Bible, supplies important insights by which to assess present reality. "Secular" resources such as anthropology, sociology, political science, psychology, and so forth, though they will not be developed in this volume, are also important in forming opinion concerning contemporary political and social issues.

Over the centuries, Christians have developed a number of theological statements regarding Israel. Many are concerned with biblical Israel. Others use the term "Israel" to refer to the church as the continuation of God's people. Many Christians have uncritically accepted these theological statements as a basis for understanding and relating to the modern nation Israel. Some Christians have been unreservedly pro-Israel, assuming that the creation of modern Israel has indisputable religious significance. Other Christians, drawing upon biblical denunciations of ancient Israel by the prophets or the apostles, have taken an equally solid stance against modern Israel, rejecting any positive theological understanding for fear of incorrectly validating Israel or its politics.

To reflect on the importance of land and to concentrate particularly on Israel, we must consider some of the theological assumptions that many Christians (and others as well) draw upon in relation to this topic. Many of their working suppositions are strongly held and filled with emotion or religious conviction. Some will be threatened and disturbed when their assertions are challenged or disputed. Nevertheless, clarification is important, and in many instances new understandings should replace previously held views.

In light of what we know about the contemporary peoples of Israel in all their diversity, the historical circumstances of the nation, and the biblical tradition, my goal in this chapter is to consider and reformulate some theological statements often heard in discussions about modern Israel and land. Errors in opinion are usually relatively easy to correct, but much more important and difficult to counter are convictions that need reconsideration in view of changed conditions. Christians believe that God's Spirit is always at work, bringing new insight and new reality to light. With this in mind, I will seek to shape a new understanding of how God and Israel are related and what this may mean with respect to land.

IS ISRAEL "ISRAEL"?

When we start thinking about modern Israel, several widespread teachings should be acknowledged and in some instances challenged. The first simply equates the modern geopolitical Israel (*Medinat Yisrael*) with the people called Israel in the Bible. While this may seem reasonable to the uncritical, there is actually no direct, obvious, unassailable reason to equate the two totally distinct historical realities any more than to equate modern Iran with ancient Persia.

Modern Israel was so named with the deliberate intention of claiming for itself the legacy of ancient Israel as the rightful reconstitution in Palestine of a long-absent people. Some Jews may actually be able to trace their lineage back to ancient Israel, though this is highly unlikely. But certainly some Jewish families can demonstrate generations of habitation in Palestine, as can some Christian Arab families. But modern Israel is a new geopolitical organization fashioned for the most part in the past fifty-eight years. That it is situated on land once occupied by another nation named Israel is true, but that does not mean that when we read "Israel" in the Bible we should automatically and rightly think of modern Israel as the continuation of that ancient people. What can be said with certainty is that modern Israel was created to provide haven for Jews and a place where Judaism could be lived without hindrance.

Judaism, it should be remembered, developed parallel to Christianity during the second and third centuries of the Common Era. Judaism emerged after the fall of Jerusalem (70 CE), largely as a continuation and development of the practices of a group known as the Pharisees. Judaism is based in part on the Bible, but even more upon traditions now preserved in the Talmud. At the time, Judaism took a form that can be regarded as the precursor of contemporary Judaism. By the decree of the Roman conquerors Jews were not allowed to live in Jerusalem and only in a few scattered places elsewhere in Palestine (mainly in the Galilee). Jews lovingly and longingly remembered Jerusalem across the centuries as the ancient center of a people from whom they were descended and as a place of unique holiness. When many Jews hear the term "Israel," they think of themselves as a direct continuation of the ancient people into modern times.

But there is too much discontinuity and there are too many changes and problems to make such a claim believable to all the many others who likewise have some connection with the ancient people and the land on which it was situated. Modern

Israel is not ancient Israel. It is a new creation and very valu-able, but not as the continuation of a nation that existed in a totally different time. Modern Israel is a place for Jews and for the expression of Judaism, but it is not the source of Judaism.

When we read the Bible, we must be quite clear that its Israel is not the modern nation. Much confusion and injustice have resulted from a failure to recognize this difference. Any rights held by biblical Israel do not belong automatically to modern Israel alone. The promises and the relationship with God claimed by biblical Israel are now part of the legacy of two peoples, both Judaism and Christianity. Obviously many Jews would not agree, but when the early Christians continued to define themselves on the basis of the Bible (at that point what we now would call the Hebrew Bible or Tanak or Old Testament), the claim was being made that Christians, too, share in all the promises received by the ancient people Israel. Thus, Christians insist that any continuing value of such testa-ments belongs to Christians as well as to Jews. This is a critical point, at least from a Christian perspective, to recognize and maintain.

IS THE CHURCH "ISRAEL"?

If modern Israel is not to be equated with biblical Israel, should the church be so designated? Did not the church become the "new Israel"? Didn't the Jews reject Jesus and in return receive the punishment and rejection of God? There are passages in the New Testament that support this view. The church long has taught this. But is it true? Can a position that has resulted in forcible expulsions, oppression, murder, and discrimination against Jews truly represent the will of God?

The claim that the church is to be equated with ancient Israel has come under increasing criticism during the past forty years. The Holocaust provided stark evidence that the church had nourished anti-Semitism over many centuries. The idea that Christianity replaced Judaism, with the church assuming the place of Israel in God's eyes, is called supersessionism. Hitler and his propagandists used such teachings to justify the "final solution," the attempted eradication of all European Jews (and if Hitler had won World War II, of all Jews). Many Christians cooperated, directly or indirectly, in the Holocaust. Many Christians, in Europe and in the United States, turned a deaf ear to Jewish cries for help. And while Eastern Christians are quick to deny any involvement on their part in the destruction of European Jewry, their history, too, is stamped by a virulent anti-Jewish attitude that began long before the founding of modern Israel and continues in many quarters today. The Christian teaching of supersessionism lies at the root of this hostility.

Can God have intended Christians to murder Jews? Does the continued existence of Judaism, despite centuries of persecution at the hands of Christians, Muslims, and others, not suggest that God still cares for Jews? Could it be that the church, after it became the state religion under Constantine in 324 CE, misappropriated a tradition that had been cast in an earlier era when the conflict between Christians and Jews was mainly between two distinct minorities within the empire (100–200 CE)? Yes, the New Testament book of Hebrews strongly points in a supersessionist direction (Heb. 8:1–13), but the issues being addressed by the writer of Hebrews had mainly to do with Christian self-identity and should not be read in a way that disparages contemporary Jews. In light of the new understandings in biblical study and with the many questions noted above, many contemporary Christians have urged a serious and immediate reconsideration of the church's teachings about Jews and Judaism. Particularly has the teaching of supersessionism come under serious question.

In the same way that it is wrong to equate modern Israel with ancient, biblical Israel, so it is not accurate to understand the church as the simple continuation of ancient Israel. Christians rightly contend that the church has a relationship with ancient Israel, but this is a relationship that the church shares with Judaism. The church alone is not God's Israel (contrary to some readings of Gal. 6:16). Divine promises to ancient Israel must now be heard in light of the emergence of two new realities, Judaism and Christianity. However Christians may think and talk about their biblical heritage, they cannot assume to own it all by themselves. Two vital communities, Judaism and Christianity, claim direct descent from those who lived by and preserved the biblical stories; a third, Islam, treasures the tradition as well.

IS GOD GATHERING "ISRAEL"?

Many Christians embrace the view that the creation of modern Israel is the fulfillment of prophecy. Such an idea can find support in Scripture, and a number of texts can be brought forward to support the position. The idea of prophecies in the Old Testament finding fulfillment in Jesus is found in the New Testament. This understanding of "fulfillment" was one of the principal grounds used in the early church to link the Old Testament with the New. Some Jews also interpret some parts of the Bible in this way to validate the existence of modern Israel. It is important to realize, in Christian circles at least, that this understanding of some Old Testament passages is based upon an interpretation of the texts usually guided by theological convictions that are not clearly and unmistakably biblical.

The simplest version of the argument among Christians is that all the words of the prophets must be fulfilled because the prophets were predicting the future. Some prophecies, the argument goes, have been fulfilled, but many have not. Among the latter is the prediction that at the end of time or at the beginning of the messianic age, the people of Israel—scattered abroad when their nation was destroyed as punishment from God—will be gathered and returned to their former land. Sometimes in this view, the return is seen as the beginning of a time when Jews will be converted to Christianity or at least will acknowledge that Jesus is Messiah. For others, the ingathering of Jews is simply a sign of the end time, when Christians will be delivered from this evil world before final judgment falls on those left behind.

On the surface, the argument is persuasive if the texts in question are read out of context and in accordance with the presupposed theology. But this is a theological claim not accepted by all. Several criticisms may rightly be lodged against this interpretation. First, the texts in their original literary and historical contexts were words of accusation and hope directed by the prophets to particular audiences of real people. These were not mysterious words of prediction that would only be understood thousands of years after they were uttered. The whole notion is based on a misunderstanding of the character and intention of the biblical prophets and their work. The biblical prophets were "forth tellers" not "foretellers."

Second, how does anyone determine what does or does not constitute fulfillment? The prophets certainly had a vision of a time when all of God's people would gather to praise God and live in peace and harmony, but can the establishment of modern Israel be the fulfillment of this grand vision? Proponents in support of this "prediction" theory often put forward end time texts from Ezekiel. Ezekiel 47 is one such passage. Ezekiel speaks of a new temple with a stream flowing from it that waters the whole land. The Dead Sea becomes fresh water; an abundance of life blossoms throughout the land. Extensive borders are described and within them land is reallocated according to the ancient tribal boundaries. Non-Jews within Israel will be given land as well. Now, this is a beautiful vision, but it certainly does not describe modern Israel. Of course, one can interpret the passage nonliterally and talk about how modern Israel has brought life to the desert through irrigation and cultivation, but such a figurative reading of the text leaves no logical basis for interpreting the text or Israel as a literal fulfillment of prophetic vision.

Finally, this fulfillment argument ignores the fact that many of the texts cited can just as well be understood as fulfilled (if one must) by the return of the exiles from Babylon in 538 BCE and the following several years. Certainly, some people in restored Jerusalem during the time of Haggai and Zechariah so understood themselves. They understood some of Isaiah's words, and some of those of the prophets Jeremiah and Ezekiel as well, as references to their own return. But to disregard the context in which these words were proclaimed, heard, and gathered is to do them damage.

Much more could be said in criticism of this position, which is vigorously advocated by some Christians known as dispensationalists and others known as premillennialists (see For Further Reading at the end of this chapter). The fundamental error, however, is to read too literally texts intended to engender hope and consolation. The words of the prophets were intended to assure God's people of ongoing divine care and compassion. They may help us articulate a theological vision, but they do not constitute a deterministic program we can use to predict God's time.

IS ISRAEL GOD'S CREATION?

Some Christians and Jews attribute the creation of the modern State of Israel directly to the hand of God. They see in it an act of divine intervention in the history of the world. Other Christians, Jews, and Muslims vehemently denounce such a view for a variety of reasons. What are we to make of this? Is it correct to say that modern Israel was created by God?

From a Christian perspective, the possibility of grave error resides in both positions. On the one hand, to say Israel is the result of direct divine intervention is to invite such unsupportable corollaries as: (1) God ordained the Holocaust to make Jews return to Palestine, or (2) God willed the suffering of hundreds of thousands of Palestinian Christians and Muslims who have been displaced by the creation of Israel. On the other hand, to say God had nothing whatsoever to do with the establishment of modern Israel and to argue that human politics alone gave rise to the Jewish state, is to suggest (1) that God has no interest or influence in the affairs of the world, and (2) that God is indifferent to human struggle and pain. Christians simply cannot settle for positions that ascribe the formation of

Israel directly to God or that assert that the creation of the Jewish state has no religious significance whatsoever.

The struggle to create a modern Israel is clearly a very human story. Political and military actions by Muslims, Christians, and Jews were very real. Nations were involved; the United Nations acted. Christians believe that God's purpose is somehow assisted and resisted through such human efforts. Thus it would be wrong to say that no religious significance accompanied the momentous establishment of modern Israel. The nation was founded, at least in part, because of the dire circumstances into which Jews had fallen at the hands of Europeans, many of whom characterized themselves as Christians. For many Jews, the haven that became Israel was their only hope for survival. Certainly this has religious significance.

Because Christians believe that God does have a stake in what human beings do, they can also insist that part of the importance of Israel rests in how Israel lives among its neighbors. In the ambiguity of human existence, the creation of Israel was marked by injustice for some while providing deliverance for others. When Jews moved in, many Palestinians had to move over or get out; inequities have occurred. While all parties involved can claim their share of atrocities, both as perpetrators and victims, it remains the burden of the government of modern Israel to act in a responsible and just manner for all within its borders. The religious significance of Israel in the longer term will be determined by how the rich ethical teaching of Judaism is embodied by the only state calling itself Jewish. Many Jews think it unfair to be judged by more rigorous norms than other nations, but Israel has set its own standard by declaring itself a Jewish state. Christians hope Israel will live by those high ideals.

One final word of warning is necessary about the issue of how to understand the fact of Israel's existence. Christians have no basis on which to claim moral superiority or divine destiny. The nations they inhabit, including the United States, have very ambiguous human origins. Violence and injustice can be found in all national histories. While Israel may warrant criticism on occasion, the misdeeds and failings of other nations should not be overlooked. Since Christians do criticize the government of Israel, they should also consider and comment upon the records of the surrounding Arab nations, many of which are totally autocratic. The human rights record in many Arab states is appalling. The failure to assimilate and provide decent living for the numerous refugees that have entered their borders is indefensible. The seeming unwillingness to negotiate legitimate peace with Israel raises questions for many who stand outside the immediate situation. Israel's Arab neighbors do not have a stellar record. Christians would do well to acknowledge this and bring their justified criticism upon all the deserving parties.

Some may believe it too much to say God created Israel, but let no one say that Israel doesn't matter to God or that Israel's life as a nation is illegitimate. Israel does exist and has provided much good for many—even though there are clearly wrongs that should be corrected. God is as concerned for Israel as for each of the other nations of the world. The modern State of Israel is important to God.

IS ISRAEL SPIRITUALLY SIGNIFICANT?

Christians are prone to adopt yet another position, expressing a preference for things that are "spiritual" and "universal" over things that are "material" and "particular." Christianity long has had a tendency to take pride in being a faith that values the "universal" over the "particular." The universal significance of Christ, for instance, is more important for many Christians than the particular, concrete, material life of Jesus. Since the very beginning of Christianity, there have been those who sought to disprove or at least de-emphasize the material character of Jesus, the realness of his humanity in all of its particularity. In this viewpoint, Jesus as the divine, spiritual manifestation of God was what was really important.

The consequences of this error are wide reaching. Rather than understand God's blessings in any way as earthly and material, Christians have often characterized them as heavenly and spiritual. Rather than address and redress the wrongs of this world, some have encouraged a passive acceptance of tyranny in expectation of an "otherworldly" or "heavenly" existence of plenty and painlessness. Material existence has too often been characterized as finite, futile, and essentially sinful. Spiritual existence, on the other hand, is touted as superior in every way, and it requires a fundamental rejection of material reality.

When one then asks about the spiritual significance of Israel, this is to some a loaded question. Undoubtedly, many Christians do not believe that modern Israel has spiritual significance. They believe that Judaism is at worst a godless perversion of the truth and at best of no more importance than any other human (that is, pagan) religious system. After all, they argue, Judaism concentrates on particulars rather than universals. By its insistence on ethnicity guarded by restricted interaction with others, Judaism, these Christians contend, misses universal truth entirely or at best distorts it. These Christians think that by concentrating on fulfilling 613 specific rules, Jews have missed the universal aim of the law. Preconceived attitudes of disdain and superiority by these Christians with respect to Jews, however, are often the real logic that guides this negative perception.

Does Israel have spiritual significance? Yes, but not in any exclusive sense. This answer should not be understood to deny or disregard the material significance of Israel or to make of it some unreal phantom in the world. Israel is, above all, a real, concrete, material state in a particular, geographically specific place in this world. Biblical tradition is rooted in the lives of specific people in particular communities. Loving God and loving neighbor cannot be realized in the abstract. Thus, for those Jews who wish to live out their understanding of obedience to God in the fullest possible way, a specific place is required. Despite the numerous difficulties, it is only in the promised land, according to the Torah, that *all* the commandments can be obeyed. Without security and some level of autonomy in Palestine, Jewish culture cannot be realized fully.

The State of Israel, therefore, does have spiritual significance, at least for Jews.

It is important, however, to go further, because for Christians ancient Israel was a "particular" that pointed beyond itself to "universals." Ancient Israel was intended, among other things, Christians believe, to provide a model of God's way for the world. God's Torah (teaching) was entrusted to ancient Israel so that humanity could understand how better to live together. How well ancient Israel succeeded in this task is not the question here, but Jews and Christians, for the most part, recognize this function as part of ancient Israel's calling. Thus, as a particular nation among nations, ancient Israel had a role that went beyond that of others.

Modern Israel, insofar as it attempts to be a Jewish state, shares some of the same burden and blessing of ancient Israel. By seeking to enable Jews, and the non-Jews in its midst, to live in accordance with God's way, some contend that the nation points beyond itself. It is not only a nation like other nations, but it has also accepted an additional objective, namely that of demonstrating in this concrete, real world the spiritual reality of God's desire that human beings live in ways that honor their creator and show respect for one another. By claiming what is at least in part a religious dimension, some see modern Israel seeking to point beyond itself, to be a light for others, to demonstrate spiritual significance in a this-world setting. Christians commend this objective and stand in awe of the effort required to live it out faithfully.

IS ISRAEL GOD'S CHOSEN?

Another claim we must consider is the notion that since ancient Israel is known in the Bible as a "chosen people," so must modern Israel be recognized as "chosen." Once again the fundamental error of identifying ancient with modern Israel comes into play. Some Christians take such an idea to mean that modern Israel is a nation of divine destiny. Others denounce any notion that only one people or one nation can be "chosen." Still other Christians contend the church is now the "chosen people" and thus "chosenness" has become less particular, less ethnic, and certainly nonmaterial.

Speaking of Israel, ancient or modern, as chosen by God must be done with great care. Certainly numerous biblical texts speak of ancient Israel as chosen. Those same texts, however, make it absolutely clear that being chosen was not based on intrinsic superiority of any kind possessed by Israel. Being chosen simply meant that ancient Israel was given a task and was held accountable. In somewhat the same way, it is indeed permissible to speak of the church as chosen.

What is most interesting, however, is that the ruler of the universe decided to relate to humanity through the medium of a very particular people. Israel was chosen to be the people/nation with which God would demonstrate divine compassion, judgment, deliverance, and all the rest. Jesus was born a Jew. The Bible presents God as one who has made commitments to a particular, worldly company and has known in detail the frailties of humankind. The God of heaven and earth, at least as far as the Bible is concerned, is not known in some abstract way. Unlike an "unmoved mover" or "ground of being," God has a name and has interacted with people from time immemorial as one who chooses and makes commitments.

It is not right to say that God has chosen modern Israel in some way different from the way God has interacted with other nations. It is correct, however, to say that, insofar as God is known by any nation, it is by God's choice. To the degree that any nation lives with a sense of being chosen by God, it can only mean that the nation is under obligation to love God and neighbor in such a way that others are directed to God. In this sense, every nation and no nation may be chosen.

While it may seem incredible to the modern world that human beings can matter so much to God, both Jews and Christians believe just that. Further, they both teach that the creator of all has risked becoming involved with particular groups as a way to reach out to all. Many modern people cannot fathom how that could work, so they conclude it cannot be what God has done (if in fact there even is a God). They insist that particular historical events and nations are simply the result of chance or causation of some indeterminable sort and thus have no real value or meaning. Biblical tradition keeps insisting, however, that God is at work in and with these events and peoples.

God has not chosen modern Israel as a nation above nations. At the same time, however, God has chosen modern Israel as a particular place where the divine claims on human life can be made concrete and visible. Also chosen in this sense is every nation where Jews and Christians dwell. Whether modern Israel has been chosen for anything more, only history will tell, for it is in history that God brings life and judgment to fruition among the nations.

IS ISRAEL'S LAND GOD-GIVEN?

Some contemporary Christians and Jews assume that Israel possesses its land by divine action. Following the same logic that has already been utilized above, such a view must be seen as erroneous. This position is defended by references to promises made by God to Abraham and Sarah, their progeny, and later to David. All the land traversed by Abraham and Sarah during their sojourn in Canaan, so the argument goes, is intended by God to belong to modern Israel. Biblical names displace modern names. Samaria and Judea are used instead of Jordan or West Bank. Palestinian Nablus is called biblical Shechem. The territory of ancient Israel is claimed as the God-given land, to be held and governed by modern Israel.

This position has several problems. First, its proponents often cite a long list of biblical passages in support of their claims. These passages, however, fall into three categories: (1) texts that were fulfilled with the entry of ancient Israel into the land (Genesis, Deuteronomy and Joshua); (2) texts that were fulfilled by the return from the Babylonian exile (e.g., passages from Isaiah,

Jeremiah, Haggai, and Zechariah); and (3) passages that refer to the end time or the last days, texts that can only be fulfilled by the appearance of a new heaven and new earth (e.g., certain passages from Isaiah, Ezekiel, Joel, and Daniel). None of these passages support land claims now! The authority of such claims, if any ever existed, was either used thousands of years ago or must await a new age. Because God may have granted land in the past to ancient Israel does not mean that modern Israel has a legal justification for occupying the land now.

The founders of modern Israel recognized this. Their efforts to buy land in Palestine, beginning in the last decades of the nineteenth century and continuing to the establishment of the current nation, are clear testimony to their understanding. The tireless political activity aimed at creating the nation also signals a realistic understanding of the ways of the world. Those who dreamed of a Jewish haven, a new Jewish state, were drawn to the fact that Jerusalem and the surrounding area were the most appropriate place, but they knew that they could not claim the land simply on the basis of prior occupancy centuries earlier. For the religious, such claims based on the Bible may make some sense, but in courts of law and in circles where human justice counts, such divine right claims to land are insufficient.

Israel does have a legal right to much of its land. It was granted this by the United Nations at the time of partition. Whether popular or not, a decision was made that allowed a new nation to be born with all the rights of nationhood. A territory was defined, and Israel assumed responsibility for defending its borders and its citizens from attack—a task it has effectively exercised.

For many years most Muslims and many Christians denounced or ignored the action of the United Nations. It is understandable that the Arab nations and the displaced Palestinians deeply resent an action by other nations that granted Israel the right to be established on what they consider Arab land. The reality, nonetheless, is that the United Nations did just that. So far as the international community is concerned, Israel is legal and has territorial rights. The irony is that this same international community offers the best hope for justice for the region's Palestinian refugees and for some resolution of the continuing dispute over borders. The United Nations has repeatedly asked for all parties to address these issues. In 1993, Israel and the Palestinians took the first steps toward a political solution, and other Arab entities moved toward an honorable peace settlement that recognizes Israel's right to secure borders. Similar efforts continue, though resolution is far from accomplished.

To repeat, the claim of some Jews and Christians that the occupied territories, especially Samaria and Judea, otherwise known as the West Bank, belong to Israel because the Bible says so has absolutely no legal weight within the international community. It is nonetheless of interest within certain religious communities and thus warrants further comment.

Claims that the land was given by God raise two important issues. First is the matter of divine promises. If God promised the land to the offspring of Sarah and Abraham, then the trustworthiness of God is on the line. God's promises must be kept or God is diminished. At one level it can be said, as was noted earlier, that the interpretation of the texts is crucial. Some argue that the promises of land and a return to land were fulfilled in ancient Israel's history or can only be kept at the end of time. Some, particularly Christians, want to argue that modern Israel's emergence is a sign of the last days. If so, then using the argument to justify the legality of territorial claims is rather moot. What's more, at this literalistic level, Christians and Muslims, it would seem, should also have a share in the land since they too are descendants of Abraham.

At a more important level, God's trustworthiness does not depend upon the vicissitudes of human politics. God was with Abraham and Sarah before they went forth. God was with Israel in the wilderness, during the Exile, and throughout the Diaspora. God can be believed whether Jews return to the land occupied by ancient Israel or not, and many Jews willingly and eloquently attest to this. God's honor is not at risk in this discussion.

The second issue raised by claims of God-given land concerns assumptions that God is involved in the affairs of human history and whether a particular place is required for the full expression of Judaism. Few people of faith argue that God is uncaring or uninvolved in human history, but wide disagreements exist over how God is engaged in these events. But does Judaism require a specific place in which to live out religious conviction? Jerusalem has long had special significance to Jews, and certain commandments can only be fulfilled there. Nonetheless, as its own history shows, Judaism does not require the establishment or continuation of modern Israel for its existence or continuation. This should not, however, diminish recognition of the importance of the renewed commitment and hope that modern Israel has brought to countless Jews. An understanding of contemporary Judaism requires the acknowledgment of the importance, both symbolically and literally, of the modern state of Israel in the self-understanding of Jews.

What is required for any person of faith is a concrete place in a real world where decision is called for and righteousness and justice can be practiced. To affirm this is to acknowledge the significance of a land promise without using it to justify political claims for autonomy over particular territory by any group. It is to insist that every group must be secure in its practice of religion and in the opportunity for a fulfilling life. If there is God-given land, it is the earth, a consideration that will be treated more fully in the concluding chapter.

INTERPRETATION AS A THEOLOGICAL TASK

As frequently noted in the preceding pages, theological assertions have arisen over the centuries to help people understand who God is and how God engages humankind. Because of the prominence of Israel in biblical tradition and the tension experienced in the first two centuries of Christianity between Jews and the church, many formulations appeared to explain how such matters fit within God's purposes. For centuries many Christians assumed these theological ideas were correct, even though they were deeply offensive and literally harmful to Jews around the world.

Christians believe that each new generation is given the task of listening again to its tradition and fashioning appropriate interpretation in light of current reality. God has brought about surprising, unexpected, humanly inexplicable things in the past and may well do so again. Old views may need to be refashioned or even discarded. Continuity is provided in the constancy of God's love, but always a new thing may appear.

In the late twentieth century, events such as the murder of six million European Jews and the establishment of modern Israel in a predominantly Arab region require a reconsideration of theological understanding. The task of interpretation is far from complete, but a start has been made. However Israel (with all the possible nuances of that term) is to be understood finally, Christians contend that God's promises are sure, God's commitments are real, and God's intentions for justice and peace remain unqualified. Good theology will emerge as historical reality and biblical witness assist people of faith in once again fashioning proper response to God's way.

QUESTIONS FOR DISCUSSION

1. How/why does the author seek to reformulate some "theological statements often heard in discussions about modern Israel and land?" What historical and biblical information is used in suggesting and defending this reformulation?
2. Can there be, as the author says, "new understanding" that replaces views once considered to be true? What examples can you think of from science, church practices, or other areas of life? What place has God's Spirit in such a process?
3. Which of the seven questions and theological reformulations most surprised you? Why? What does the author con-

sider it appropriate to say theologically about modern Israel? The church? Do you agree or disagree? Why?

4. In the last paragraph of the chapter the author states: "Christians contend that God's promises are sure, God's commitments are real, and God's intentions for justice and peace remain unqualified." What does that statement mean to you in light of the material presented in the chapter? Is it justified? Does it need to be qualified? How can the Bible and historical review help?

FOR FURTHER READING

On the Relation of Christians and Jews

Burge, Gary M. *Whose Land? Whose Promise? What Christians Are Not Being Told about Israel and the Palestinians.* Cleveland: Pilgrim Press, 2003.

Falk, Randall M. *Jews and Christians: A Troubled Family.* Nashville: Abingdon Press, 1990.

Gager, John G. *The Origins of Anti-Semitism.* New York: Oxford University Press, 1983.

Ruether, Rosemary R. *Faith and Fratricide: The Theological Roots of Anti-Semitism.* San Francisco: Seabury Press, 1974.

A Theological Understanding of the Relationship Between Christians and Jews. Louisville, KY: Office of the General Assembly, Presbyterian Church (U.S.A.), 1987.

The Theology of the Churches and the Jewish People. New York: World Council of Churches Publications, 1988.

On Dispensationalism and Premillennialism

Ariel, Yaakov. *On Behalf of Israel: American Fundamentalist Attitudes toward Jews, Judaism, and Zionism, 1865–1945.* Brooklyn: Carlson Press, 1991.

Cox, William E. *An Examination of Dispensationalism.* Philadelphia: Presbyterian and Reformed Publishing House, 1963.

Eschatology: The Doctrine of Last Things. Materials Distribution Center, Presbyterian Church in the United States, 1978.

Weber, Timothy P. *Living in the Shadow of the Second Coming: American Premillennialism, 1875–1982*. Chicago: University of Chicago Press, 1987.

On the Place of Jerusalem and Israel for Jews

Heschel, Abraham Joshua. *Israel: An Echo of Eternity*. New York: Farrar, Straus & Giroux, 1987.

Hoffman, Lawrence A. *The Land of Israel: Jewish Perspectives*. South Bend, IN: University of Notre Dame Press, 1986.

Rudin, James A. *Israel for Christians*. Minneapolis: Fortress Press, 1983.

5

A Vision and a Challenge

A Call to Earth Keeping
and Just Reconciliation

On the basis of the preceding, very particular historical, biblical, and theological review centering on Israel and the land of Palestine, both a wider vision and a challenge emerge. The particulars suggest some broad general conclusions. At the same time, they push us to attempt to find a concrete path to reconciliation amid all the conflicting claims. A guiding theological vision that emerges from this discussion may give direction when disputes over land ownership and land use occur, but it may not be immediately obvious. The theology of land proposed in this study implies very concrete social responsibilities extending to the people who live on the land. The shape of this theology and the ethical demands it presses are the subject of this chapter.

But first, a word about wider visions. They are often fuzzy around the edges. Some would prefer detailed plans, concrete blueprints, or at least clear guidelines. Ambiguity is difficult to tolerate in the best of circumstances and becomes problematic in bad situations. Nonetheless, on the basis of this study I will present a theological vision, with the difficulties attendant to doing so. There are no guarantees, no foolproof schemes, only a vision.

Yet such a vision can do several things. It can help us to identify false claims and those things that don't ring true or sit well in light of the vision. A vision can inspire continued struggle even against great odds and keep those who embrace the vision from being satisfied with substitutes. A theological vision should spark dissatisfaction with injustice and inequity while beckoning toward a reality that may not yet be but will surely come. Those who have been grasped by such a theology may become the engineers, the builders, the problem solvers needed for addressing particular situations. But without a vision, all too often nothing happens to overcome the extraordinary power of inertia.

I will present a vision here, a guide on the basis of which to work. The vision is not the property of any one group or any one religion. The theological vision is intended to unite, not divide. And most importantly, the vision presented here requires human participation. The vision cannot and will not be imposed by God or by anyone else. Human beings must willingly accept responsibility and become active earth keepers if the vision is to shape reality effectively. Religion, as a social reality quite apart from theological reflection, will always have a role. This vision insists that religion must become a source of reconciliation and justice if we as human beings are to reach the intended goal.

This guiding vision is not based on any stunning new discoveries. Rather, the current political, economic, and social circumstances facing the inhabitants of earth prompt the imperative advanced here. Care of planet Earth and just solutions to the many conflicts sapping the resources of so many nations and communities have moved to the top of the list of "problems to be solved." Responsible care of the earth and dedicated efforts at reconciliation emerge from this study as two equally important imperatives for concrete action that should guide those who care about our common quality of life and who desire to participate in God's way.

THE BASIC PREMISE: GOD THE CREATOR

The theological vision illumined by this study is clear. God, as creator, is the only legitimate owner of the earth/land. God has placed humankind in Garden-Earth and expects us to be earth keepers who will enjoy and maintain the earth in order that all may know God's peace (*shalom*), a peace that is characterized by justice and equity for all.

As the creator, God has rightful claim on Earth, a claim that no human individual or government can invalidate. Planet Earth belongs to God. As creator, God can and has set the rules and intends that human beings will respect and live within them. Earth is to be responsibly tended as a luxurious garden for the benefit of the whole human family. Earth is not to be exploited by or for anyone. Earth, God's good land, has been placed in human hands by a loving creator who desires that all peoples live in harmony and prosperity—that is, in *shalom*, peace. With this vision, earth keepers seek to follow God's way and find in the vision a source of encouragement and renewal, and a call to just reconciliation.

This is clearly a vision based upon faith. No one can prove the truth of this vision. No one can demonstrate God's reality to the satisfaction of the skeptical or cynical. Nonetheless, those who believe that God has created the earth and all that is in it have been given a vision of how to live. Christians share this vision with others, particularly with Jews and Muslims. To be sure, variations in the specifics exist, but the fundamental agreement on the vision is most important. Earth keepers do not own the vision. Rather, they are owned by it. The guiding vision is simple enough, at least to see if not to follow. This vision has numerous implications, however, and we will now examine some of them.

A PURPOSEFUL CREATION

In antiquity, no one questioned whether God existed or whether God was the creator. There were numerous rivals to the title of "creator," but human beings, for the most part, unquestioningly assumed that the creator was a deity not to be confused with the creatures fashioned by divine power. Among religious traditions, disputes occurred over which "God" was creator, but there was little or no debate about the reality of a creator god.

Belief that God exists and that God is creator is not so automatic anymore. In rejecting rampant superstition and the spiritual and mental slavery that often accompanied it, belief in God has also been cast aside in some cases. While perhaps not denying divine reality altogether, many people in the industrialized nations go about their daily lives as if no God existed. Decisions, values, goals, relationships—life is lived without any specific reference to God. Practically speaking, God does not exist for many such people.

As already noted, the existence of God cannot be proved conclusively. No absolutely convincing argument can be made, nor will a logical syllogism win the day. It may, of course, help to press people to admit where their reason or experience necessarily must give way to premise or supposition. And after all, premise and supposition are other words for assumptions about life that often remain incompatible with absolute proof. Still, the reality of God cannot be proved, only believed and allowed to shape life.

Christianity, Judaism, and Islam share the conviction that God created Earth purposefully. Creation was not an accident. God determined to create the universe and to assign its care to humankind. Attempts to ascribe creation to some lesser deity or simply to a cosmic accident have regularly been rejected in favor of reaffirming that God responsibly and intentionally created all that is. Such a conviction is clearly supported by the Bible and the theological traditions of each of these faith communities.

But the adherents of these religions who self-consciously seek to be guided by the vision of God and God's way should not assume that a statement of their belief in God will automatically make allies or settle disputes in today's world. In fact, faith statements often cause more suspicion than good will.

Too many crimes against people and land have been committed in the name of God.

Today, those who care for the earth and who seek just remedy for conflicts involving the stewardship of land clearly include people who are not of religious faith. Nonetheless, they share at least some part of the vision for their own set of reasons. What seems certain is that all earth keepers must demonstrate their convictions in the way they live rather than by the speeches they make. That is probably the only strategy that has the possibility of effectively enlisting others in implementing the theological vision being here espoused. Abstract theology will not be enough.

GOD'S EARTH A SACRED TRUST

In itself, the earth is not holy or sacred. The earth is God's creation; God alone is holy. God is to be worshiped, not the earth. Similarly, human beings are God's creatures and in no way divine. Certain places may be regarded by some as holy because God's interaction with humankind is commemorated there, but this is only a functional sacredness and not absolute. Certain people may be set aside as holy for special holy tasks, but they too have only a derived holiness. Creatures and the created can point to God's holiness, but they do not in themselves become holy. Humankind has value and life because the holy God, the creator, so wills.

Sometimes "religious" people make claims that go beyond even their own traditions. There are those who worship the earth and ascribe godlike attributes to it. For Christians, the earth may at times be called "Mother Earth," but that is not intended to deify the earth but to acknowledge human connection with and dependence upon the earth as our only material source of sustenance. Christians do not worship the earth, the stars, or any other parts of God's creation. Only God is holy.

That earth is not rightly regarded as holy, however, does not mean that it is valueless or that humans can use it for any purpose. God created humankind and gave human beings the very important tasks of worshiping God and caring for God's land and for one another. As humans till Garden-Earth, they are provided nourishing food and beautiful surroundings. As they care for one another, they further exercise another important dimension of their stewardship. God never intended that human beings should arrogantly presume that they could do anything they please with God's good land. Exploiting or wasting earth's resources is irresponsible and a violation of God's trust.

This does not mean that every property-development project or every act that alters the environment is automatically to be judged as wrong. Rather, on the basis of our theological vision we must recognize that the world does not ultimately belong to any particular group of humans and certainly not only to the most powerful communities. Humans have been given a charge to care for Garden-Earth, benefit from it, and pass it to the next generation in such a way that all will be able to understand and celebrate the wonder of God's gift to humankind. For Christians this is fundamental to the vision we are to live by.

Our human record as earth keepers, particularly during the past two centuries, is not good. In the name of progress and with a desire for personal or national gain, or both, all manner of destructive exploitation has been sanctioned and carried out. The incredible polluting of Eastern Europe and China, for instance, that has come to light in recent years provides a vivid image of how much harm can be done. Israel, Saudi Arabia, Syria, and Iran, for instance—and even more, by reason of their size and capacity to affect the environment, the United States, France, Germany, Japan, and Russia—all are responsible before God. The larger industrialized nations, in some instances, seem to be coming to a new understanding of the ecological crises that are on the horizon, but they still have a long way to go to correct the damage already inflicted.

A purposeful approach is needed to guide the responsible use of the world's resources for the benefit of all. Humans are to care for Earth! Water, air, and soil are to be shared and enjoyed, not hoarded, polluted, used wastefully, or for the advantage of one over another. God's earth may not be sacred in itself, but it is a sacred trust given into human care. This is a direct corollary of the theological vision outlined here.

GOD'S EARTH KEEPERS

The Bible's opening chapters are devoted to God, God's creating acts, and the relationship of God with the creation. A special relationship is described between God and humankind. Female and male are together created in God's image and are made capable of interacting with one another and with God. According to the Bible, humankind was uniquely created and is distinct from all other creatures. Humans, the divine image bearers, have been given responsibility for the whole of creation. Genesis 1 and 2 are remarkable in their presentation of the importance and place of humanity from God's perspective.

Several things are especially important to note. The opening chapters of Genesis are not about the single people Israel. They concern all humankind—the whole human family—and the wider creation to which all humans belong. Certainly, ancient Israel remembered the Genesis accounts as prelude to their national history, but in themselves these chapters present a wider scene, a global scene, and insist that all humankind be understood as God's creation. Thus from the Bible's point of view, all humans have the same God, the only God of the universe, as their creator. Human acknowledgment or lack thereof does not alter this reality. The affirmation that God, the God of the Bible, is creator of all humankind is foundational.

Genesis makes another more subtle point. Human beings are made in God's image and likeness (Gen. 1:26–27). The Hebrew terminology used here is rather technical. Most often the Hebrew word rendered "image," for instance, refers to a statue or symbol of a ruler. Ancient rulers put up images of themselves as reminders of who was in charge. As well as erecting idols of the gods they worshiped, conquerors would place their own images at the borders of a vanquished country or in the center of a captured city as signs of ownership. From the standpoint of Genesis, human beings as made in God's image stand as living reminders of the ruler of all, the creator.

The creation belongs to God, and every human being carries the divine image as testimony throughout the earth to the fact of God's priority. Later Christian theology developed interpretations suggesting that the image of God was the human soul or mind, which enabled humans to be like God or to reflect God's Spirit. The original language, however, probably meant something much more direct. Created in God's image meant that human beings were given the responsibility of representing God in the midst of God's creation. That is still our task.

As already noted, however, humankind has not been given license to do anything it wills. Care of the creation and for one another is the main agenda. Protestant Christianity, particularly, by its largely uncritical support of emerging capitalism in the eighteenth and nineteenth centuries, carries a special burden. By espousing a view then that the biblical instruction to "fill the earth and subdue it" (Gen. 1:28) meant that humans could do just about anything they pleased with the earth and earth's creatures, Protestant Christianity indirectly supported much exploitation and waste.

Today, there is a growing awareness that the previous interpretation of God's directive was wrong. As representatives of God, humans are expected to show the same regard and care for the earth that God does. The creation was "good" and brought delight to God. Humans, who stand in God's image, are responsible to the Ruler, to the God of the Universe. The creator God is one who loves the world so much that nothing will be allowed to destroy the relationship of creator and creature. Christians believe that that love became incarnate in Jesus of Nazareth for the sake of all.

One other comment is in order here. In the picture presented by Genesis and affirmed in other places in the Bible, all human beings are designated as earth keepers. No one is exempt. All stand in God's image, and all carry a common charge. No one bears special responsibility or privilege in this regard. Israel was not assigned this special task. Israel's history may give testimony to God's intention and God's unwillingness to let human negligence or rebellion have the last word, but being earth keepers is not the peculiar task of Israel. The tending of creation, the caring, loving tilling of Garden-Earth, is intended as the work of all humankind. The question is not whether one will be an earth keeper. Rather, the question is whether one will be a good earth keeper. The theological vision assigns to all the role of earth keepers and then provides instruction on what good earth keepers will do.

Christians, Jews, and Muslims, because of the tradition we share, should strive moreover to articulate the vision and find, cooperate with, and form coalitions with, any who share the aims of the vision and are striving to fulfill it as good earth keepers. Detailed action is often difficult to plan. Negotiation regarding the most important matters, the priorities, is imperative. This is not easy, but it is part of our challenge.

GOD'S ALLOCATION OF LAND

According to the biblical view, each individual and each group need a place, a land, a part of the earth, for support and development. In the Bible, God is described as allocating land for each of the peoples of earth. Such a notion becomes hopelessly complex if any attempt is made to adopt such an allocation literally within the modern context. Metaphorically, though, the point is clear. Land is essential, for humans to have a full life. People need space, a place where they can be who they are to be. In industrialized cultures, individual land ownership may be severely reduced, with personal belongings only symbolic of this basic need. Nonetheless, people continue to live in communities, ethnic and national, which declare and press their desire for their own land.

The difficulty comes, obviously, when the claims of one person or group conflict with the claims of another. Within modern Israel, for instance, conflicting claims have created great tension and strife, as some would put it, between long-resident Arabs and newly arrived Jews. Or as others would describe it, the tension is between people of God-given legacy over against uncooperative resisters. These same kinds of difficulties are found around the world in places like Bosnia, Ireland, Azerbaijan, Guatemala, and even between some communities within the United States.

From the standpoint of the theological vision developed here, the claim of a God-given right to land is invalid unless it includes the conviction that others also have the same God-given right to land. The tradition of God's allotment of land is important as an assertion of God's fundamental intention that all people have a place, a land. But it cannot be used to settle particular boundary claims. Such disputes require careful, rigorous negotiations aimed at the best and most just resolution possible. That all people deserve land, however, is part of the theological vision and should be kept clearly in mind.

GOD'S ABSOLUTE CLAIM

An essential platform of the biblical theological vision of land being articulated here is the conviction that the earth is God's possession alone. This necessarily implies that no individual or nation can claim absolute ownership of territory. God's land claim alone is primary and absolute. At best, humans have only secondary rights. All are living on someone else's land, God's land. Humans occupy places for shorter or longer periods of time, but they never truly own them. Humans use space wisely or stupidly, for the well-being of all or selfishly for their own interests, to build up or to tear down, but whether they acknowledge it or not, they have no absolute right to their land. Earth—all of it—was created by God and belongs to God, who instructs human beings to live on it responsibly and peacefully.

The absolute claim of God that overrides all other claims is difficult for many people to recognize or accept. Because many do not believe in God, they are not prone to accept that they can hold only secondary rights to land. Some who do not believe in God, however, do acknowledge that the earth belongs to all humankind rather than only to the powerful or lucky. While not espousing the theological vision presented here, they do share the aims. Thus, they can and should certainly become good allies in the struggle for a just allocation of land.

It is worth considering that some earth keepers, seeking to follow their understanding of the biblical vision, may have to risk giving up their own land claims to set an example for others. Given human propensity toward greed and selfishness, voluntary acts of self-denial are difficult and dangerous. Nonetheless, some may have to adjust their claims in the light of God's absolute claim. This is demonstrated early in Genesis when Abraham and Lot both acquire land. Whether, following Abraham's example, the less fertile is taken instead of the more fertile (Gen. 13:8–13), what is important is that each person should have his own land. The vision is for all to be treated more equitably, for all to enjoy some portion of God's good land.

LIVING IN *SHALOM*

On the basis of our theological vision, God's intention is that all people will live in *shalom*, in peace. Milk and honey, the messianic banquet, the end of pain and suffering—all of these biblical images are part of the picture drawn to explain God's desires for the human family. Earth is fertile and productive. With proper stewardship, all may be adequately fed and enjoy clear water and fresh air. Garden-Earth, the blue planet, has, at least for now, sufficient resources. Thus far, however, proper conduct by earth keepers has been lacking. Call it the result of sin (as Christians usually do) or obstinate stupidity (as others might prefer), too many among the human family have chosen to ignore God's vision for the earth and have pursued much more selfish and shortsighted interests. Earth can provide, but not indefinitely. Earth keepers are expected to live responsibly and peacefully.

What does it mean to live responsibly and peacefully? Is it impossibly difficult? Not from the biblical point of view. As creator, God can and has set the standard: justice. In the Bible, justice is the result of people doing what they are required or expected to do on the basis of defined relationships. People who honor their commitments to one another are righteous and their acts are just. The same applies in relationship with God. If humans live righteously, they will exploit neither the earth nor one another. If they make justice their aim, they will be sensitive to and supportive of the least among them, particularly the homeless and the poor (Lev. 19:9–10; Deut. 24:17–22). In the Bible, responsible use of land is defined directly in terms of doing justice, loving mercy, and maintaining a respectful relationship with God. Caring for the land and for one another is the standard by which land occupancy is measured.

Time is running out for earth keepers. Science suggests that Garden-Earth may well survive, but without some dramatic changes in behavior, the humans God placed in it to care for and enjoy it may not. God does not desire the extinction of humankind, but humans may do it to themselves. Good earth keepers must become messengers of *shalom* if humankind is to survive and fulfill its appointed destiny. Christians, Jews, and Muslims need to cease fighting and begin working for the good of Garden-Earth. If ever a time existed when ethnic or religious self-interest made sense or could be justified, that time is past. Today all must work together. The strong must defend the interests of the weak. Justice is the way to *shalom*, a peace that all desire and for which all have been created. Our theological vision points the way.

SPECIFIC CHALLENGES

The theology of land developed here is applicable to any particular set of circumstances. The same general theological convictions should be pertinent no matter what the situation. Specific solutions will not be provided by the vision, but general guidelines will be. Since this vision has been developed by reflecting directly upon ancient Israel, modern Israel, and the view of and role of land involved therein, it seems important to return to some of the specific challenges posed by the current historical realities encountered in modern Israel to see how the theology works. At least five areas of concern are obvious to all observers and need to be addressed: security, borders, reparation, water rights, and human rights.

First, the issue of security. It goes without saying that a significant level of security is prerequisite for an adequate life. This is one of the primary corollaries of the land theology developed above. Absolute security cannot be provided to anyone, but people should not have to worry about whether to go shopping or ride a bus for fear of attack. Neither should people have to live under military rule that by its very nature has to be faceless to some degree and is prone to abuse even under the best of circumstances. Both Israeli and Palestinian citizenry deserve more security than has prevailed in Israel and the Occupied Territories, particularly during the past thirty years. This issue has been a concern in Israel since its founding.

The theology of land outlined here leaves little doubt that all involved warrant the development of a fair apparatus for security. Building the barrier between Israeli and Palestinian population concentrations might work, but walls in themselves seldom solve problems. The real culprit is the deep antagonism that has developed between the parties. In some fashion that animosity has to be remedied. All parties must be convinced that all have the same rights and the same needs for security.

Presently the capacity to harm one another is high. Israel is the best militarily armed nation in the Middle East. It is well able to produce much of its own armament and has a ready source of backup in the United States. At the same time, various armed militias among the Palestinians, especially Hamas in the West Bank and Gaza and Hezbollah in Lebanon and Syria, continue to receive military supplies from the several Arab nations surrounding Israel. Security for the peoples in Israel and the Occupied Territories seems unlikely until outside sources of armaments are eliminated. Israel's military will still have an advantage, but international pressure should be effective if the active threat of missile attacks, suicide bombings, and the like is significantly reduced or totally removed. One place to begin, then, is to work for the overall reduction of the availability of arms in the region with a concurrent guarantee by the international community of security. There is obvious risk, but there is considerable risk in the status quo.

Hand in hand with the issue of security is the second challenge, the matter of borders. Defensible borders are clearly the first line of defense needed in establishing a secure environment. The quest for the fair definition of the national boundaries has been a part of Israel's life from the very beginning. Our theological vision does not allow for a solution to this concern simply by claiming some sort of divine right to land. The Bible does not provide land title to any one group. But borders are part and parcel of national existence.

There is no easy solution to this issue. Negotiations are desperately needed. The place to begin, as various peace efforts have suggested, is with the "green line" that was in place before the 1967 war. Israel has shown a willingness to accept this definition of a border, though not without some significant alterations, particularly around Jerusalem. Before his stroke, Sharon seemed to be moving in this direction. In recent years the Palestinian Authority in the occupied territories, led by Fatah, has also acknowledged Israel's legal right to the boundaries in effect from 1948 to 1967, based on the actions of the United Nations. Whether Hamas will at some point move to this position is yet to be determined.

But the discrepancies between the green line of 1948 and the actual occupation line of 2006 will be difficult to work out. For the Palestinians the aim should be to make certain that communities now divided by the actual or proposed barrier would be reunited. Trades for land now occupied by some of the settlements around Jerusalem are due. A secure border with Israel is necessary. There should be a fair reallocation of territory, to such extent as is possible. Israel will need to give up some areas now occupied, and Palestinians will have to accept less than they want in order to gain more than they presently have. Our theology of land supports this difficult project.

But we expect a degree of justice that goes beyond international standards, on the basis of the biblical tradition that informs the theological vision articulated here. Biblical justice includes setting things right so that reconciliation may be possible. This brings us to the third challenge, the question of reparation for the many Palestinians and Jews displaced in 1948 and again in 1967. Individual Palestinians have lost much as a result of the wars between the Arab nations and Israel. This is true for the many Jews forced to relocate as well. It would seem that some acknowledgment of the losses of the individuals in each group is in order and that some form of reparation should be worked out. For any resolution to be accomplished, however, Palestinians will have to put away their "all or nothing" stance and work *with* the Israelis and not always *against* them. Some form of reciprocal compensation for land and property lost is understandable within the theology of land that has been elaborated here.

The issue of a just reparation for property lost is often connected to allowing Palestinians the same "right of return" offered to Jews. Any Jew from any nation can move to Israel and claim citizenship and all the rights of a citizen. Some argue that displaced Palestinians should have the same right. Of course, if this were allowed and if any significant number of Palestinians exercised such an option, the makeup of Israel's population would be dramatically changed. Israel could not continue as both a Jewish state and as a democracy. Since no Israeli government is ever likely to accept such an arrangement, insistence on a "right of return" provision in peace efforts assures failure for any effort at negotiation.

A fourth issue, water rights, is technical and can only be mentioned here in general terms. The need for a place, a land, necessarily includes the right to have a share in water resources available in the area. Some so-called neutral observers have studied this issue for several decades and have regularly issued

reports indicting Israeli civil and military authorities for divert-
ing or withholding water from Arab communities and their
fields. The great need for water by the large urban areas of Israel
and by the extensive Israeli agricultural system is obvious. How
to share the somewhat limited water resources is not so clear.
This is an issue that needs careful review and attention. Our
theological vision requires a just resolution to this land-related
concern, but it will be necessary to have water experts—Israeli,
Palestinian, and others—actively involved in such negotiations.

Finally, the matter of the human rights of persons living in
the Occupied Territories and also of Israeli Arabs (Muslim and
Christian) is of great concern. Israel's military rule should be
judged by international standards, as would that of any nation.
By such a standard Israel's military rule has been more humane
than many military occupations in history. Nonetheless it is
military rule, and careful scrutiny is in order.

The reported abuses of Palestinians by Israeli military personnel—and these are too numerous and too well documented
simply to be dismissed—raise serious questions. Further, a significant number (though difficult to document) of Arab Christians
have left the region, citing discrimination by Israeli authorities.
Because of Israel's self-definition as a Jewish state, a stronger measure of justice is perhaps expected of Israel than might otherwise be
the case. Lapses of individual judgment or national policy in this
regard dishonor Israel. Such concerns have been frequently
addressed by the Israeli Supreme Court, which has regularly dis-
played deep respect for the rule of law and for the protection of
individual rights. The ongoing attention of the Israeli citizenry
and the Israeli government for such matters is imperative.

But any measure of judgment leveled at Israel should also be
applied to other peoples and governments in the region. Palestinians, while having a right to a secure land in which to live
and develop their culture, are also subject to the same judgment. Attacks launched by Palestinians against Palestinians
charged with collaboration have happened far too often. The
struggle between armed factions within the Palestinian community—between Fatah and Hamas for instance—do not aid

in establishing a secure setting. The refusal of Arab nations to offer much help beyond military assistance to the Palestinians is unacceptable. And of course, Palestinians have been responsible for the death of numerous Israeli citizens, combatant and noncombatant alike. All of these issues need to be addressed by Palestinians with Palestinians.

Human rights issues associated with land claims are not the unique problem of Israel. In many parts of the globe, war and exploitation are carried out under the banner of land claims. The indigenous peoples of Central America, the Muslim populations in the former Yugoslavia, and the people of Tibet are some of many who have been systematically attacked and killed over land disputes and claims. The slaughter of Native Americans in North America in the nineteenth century, the massacre of 1.8 million Armenians by the Turks between 1894 and 1918, and Hitler's attempt to exterminate the Jews are so hideous that one would think the world would learn and turn to God's way of responsibility and peace based on justice for all. But so far, this has not happened.

Residents of modern Israel and the areas currently controlled by Israel all have a right to secure land in which to live and develop their cultures. In trying to assist in the settlement of land disputes, the recognition of divine intention is most important. The best stance will usually be that the rights and responsibilities of all parties will be recognized, rather than claims made for only one and not the other. How can Jews and Muslims and Christians live together in one place? How can the hopes of each group be acknowledged and honored? What compromises are necessary? Possible? Some individuals or groups will probably need to serve as mediators striving to bring about a just resolution and reconciliation. In the final analysis, the guiding vision insists that God has allotted the earth to humankind and has given human beings the necessary intelligence to work out the details. The needs and dreams of each person and group are at stake when anyone is deprived unjustly.

Good earth keepers cannot rest until just solutions are found and implemented. Formal negotiations have been initiated at the international level, and these are good. But local efforts are perhaps even more important. In Israel various "peace parties" that have included Christians, Jews, and some Muslims, have sought, for instance, to lessen tensions by bringing Muslim and Jewish teenagers together in order to let individuals of one group meet individuals of the other. In a few places, Arab and Jewish communities within Israel have purposely developed relationships built around a sharing of agricultural products and a celebration of shared achievements. Such strategies for beginning to address these vital land-related issues are to be commended.

A WORD OF CAUTION

A special word of caution to Christians is in order. Some seventeen million Christians reside in the countries of the Middle East, a small portion of them in Israel. In almost every place they constitute a very small minority community. These Christians often live in rather precarious circumstances and are certainly not in a position to protest effectively the political realities they, with others, may face. They have had some freedom to raise their voices in Egypt, Lebanon, and Israel, but their impact has been minimal, as would be expected. For the most part, they have to concentrate on their day-to-day existence. Their hope in terms of human assistance is in the worldwide church, most of which is situated outside the Middle East.

Thus, Western Christians, among others, have a special responsibility to work for justice and reconciliation among the peoples of the Middle East. But special care should be taken to resist siding with one particular group over another. Christians need to advocate justice equally for all the people involved, something obviously easy to say and difficult to do. Some Christians in the West have too frequently offered vigorous, uncritical, unqualified support for the government of Israel, either out of their own mistaken apocalyptic/dispensational theology or for fear of being considered anti-Jewish. Others seemed to take an equally one-sided approach totally for the

Palestinians, regardless of the Palestinian rhetoric of hate and animosity against Israel, a position these Christians justify because of the Christians in the region, some of whom are Palestinians. This is especially important for Christians to recognize.

Our theological vision requires more. Yes, there may be occasions when one side or the other needs a direct word of reprimand or praise. But we in the West need to remember that we are outsiders. We do have Christian sisters and brothers living amid Jewish and Muslim populations in the Middle East, but we are not there ourselves. Our best efforts will come when we diligently form partnerships with Jews and Muslims to try to understand and fashion effective joint efforts at reconciliation and justice. A word of criticism of Israeli policy, for instance, will be much more effective if it comes from a coalition of Christians and Jews, rather than from a Christian group alone. A word to the Palestinian Authority will have a different ring if Christians and Muslims together voice it. Such coalitions are not easily formed or maintained. Considerable sharing and dialogue is required. But if we are to play an appropriate role in the Middle East toward the goal of better implementing our theological vision concerning the land, a joint approach is essential.

NO EASY WAY

Christians believe that human beings are given freedom and responsibility; humans are not puppets, automatons programmed for unthinking, uncaring, irresponsible existence. Rather, human beings have been created with the capacity to discern and to choose better over worse. They don't always do what they are capable of doing—indeed, they often ignore or renounce their own capacities. Nonetheless, humans are not invariably bound to make the wrong choice, either.

When reflecting upon land and its significance, its availability, and its necessity, humans will always be tempted to be partisan, narrow-minded, grasping, defensive, and suspicious. After all, human history offers numerous examples of land being taken by one group at the expense of another. People certainly cannot afford to forget history or be overly optimistic when assessing the likelihood of human charity. Christians know about sin and the destructiveness it brings. Humans seem to be especially vulnerable to sin when it comes to land, probably because they recognize how very important land is.

The goal and hope is to be led by the vision of God's intention. God desires justice among peoples so that all may prosper in peace. Humans must continue to remind themselves and others that the earth belongs to God and only secondarily is given into the care of human beings, earth keepers. Earth is not holy, but neither is it to be used in an exploitative, destructive fashion. Humans are expected to live in ways that bring wholeness to as many as possible. Further, they should never be satisfied until all are able to live life fully in God's good land. And yes, reconciliation of Christians with Muslims and Jews, of Israelis with Arabs, of all the involved parties—that too is part of the guiding vision, the basis of hope.

But, as always, a note of cautious realism is in order. In their work *Israel, the Impossible Land*, Jean-Christophe Attias and Esther Benbassa make the following observations:

> The adoption of the theme [sacralization of the land] by secular politicians arises from a manipulation that makes the situation inextricable. You can't negotiate over the sacred. So will it have to be God who puts an end to the murderous conflict that each day only grows more inflamed? How can one live in peace in this land of men and women while anticipating salvation from on high? The over sacralization of the land, which is just as much the case among Palestinians as Israelis, particularly since the second Intifada, can only fan the conflagration there, if not spread it elsewhere, to anywhere Jews and Muslims are in close contact with each other. For the politicians, the sacred has become a political weapon, which is, moreover, inevitably turned against those who use it.
>
> It is time to disentangle the ideal Israel of those who observe the commandments from the Israel of compromise

in which Israelis seeking peace want to live. And for the Palestinians, too, it comes down to uncoupling the sacrality of the imagined land from political self-affirmation. Only recourse to the political means (even if imperfect) that democratic countries know how to use will allow the Palestinians to found the state to which they aspire, within recognized borders. The sacred cannot be divided. The land can. (Pp. 239–40)

CONCLUSION

The guiding vision I articulate in this book is simple, yet demanding. Human beings across the centuries and in a variety of cultures have shown a deep desire for and attachment to land. Claims and counterclaims have been made to justify conquests and occupations. The need for concrete, this-world space seems essential for human communities. A genuine search for ways to deal with disputes and tension is also imperative. The responsible sharing of God-created and God-owned land is the issue.

A method of analysis is suggested here. Because I assume theological convictions, some will find the approach unsatisfactory. Christians find at least three types of information especially important for the process of fashioning theological vision: (1) historical reality, (2) biblical accounts and imagery, and (3) creedal and doctrinal constructs.

Historical reality is the first critical ingredient. What has actually happened? What in fact exists? Although they debate how God interacts with human beings in the historical process, Christians agree that the history of humankind here on this very real planet Earth is important to God. God's arena is within real history on the real Earth. Thus, reflection begins here.

The second ingredient, the Bible, supplies essential data, providing a perspective by which to interpret and evaluate ongoing experience. Biblical accounts are time-conditioned, meaning that they were addressed to specific historical situations and real people in those situations. Nevertheless, the Bible offers both examples of how God and people have related and paradigms of how humans may expect God to act and how God has directed human beings to live. The Bible usually does not offer specific solutions for modern-day problems, but within it are numerous examples of the way similar issues were addressed.

Finally, creedal statements and doctrinal deductions inform Christians. A vast corpus of material has been developed reflecting on a wide variety of concerns that the church has faced across two millennia. That is important to remember. What the church believes is thus to be considered seriously. But equally important is the conviction that the formation of theology is ever ongoing. This book seeks to make a contribution to that enterprise.

On the basis of reflection rooted in historical reality, biblical accounts and imagery, and theological construction related to the emergence of the modern State of Israel, I have sought to present a rather encompassing position. Concern for a particular place, Israel, and for the struggles of the people living there, has led to insights about that particular situation. That work has in turn suggested a stance by which similar issues in many parts of the world might be approached.

The guiding vision is simple, yet demanding. God has created the earth and thereby has claim as the only legitimate owner of the land. God has created human beings in the divine image and has appointed them earth keepers, responsible for tilling and sharing Garden-Earth and for living together in mutual care. God's intention is that humankind will enjoy and preserve the beauty and fecundity of the earth for the good of all who now, or in the future, will inhabit God's good land. The way to the peace, *shalom*, that God intends is through justice and equity. While not always easy to accomplish, this theological vision assures all of the appropriateness and possibility of such a peace.

Earth keepers are given the option of following God's way or rejecting it. God's way is marked by compassion for the weak and vulnerable, regard for justice and equity, and acknowledgment of the genuine need of each person for a safe place to live and flourish. Good earth keepers will accept the challenge to use God-given intellect and skill to develop and implement strategies for *shalom*. The adjustment of individual lifestyles as well as the analysis and transformation of human systems will be matters of concern and cooperation. Reconciliation of conflicting parties will be necessary.

For some, the establishment of modern Israel has been proclaimed the herald of the Messianic Age. In view of biblical statements and historical reality, such claims seem extravagant. It seems better to see the creation of Israel as the result of political events that may have religious significance but not as a part of a mysterious, divine plan loaded with mystical meaning. The history of Israel dramatizes the needs of human communities for secure land while also concretely illustrating the conflicts that often surround land claims and land acquisition. Any serious consideration of the significance of the struggle for land in Israel will eventually lead to consideration of other peoples as well, and other land disputes, each concretely different and yet so similar.

Some have called the establishment of modern Israel a miracle. Such a label is accurate on at least one count. The primary function of miracles in the Bible is to point beyond the miraculous to the God who is their source. The miracle of Israel does point beyond itself with a strong reminder that the world is to be understood as belonging to God. The fact of modern Israel has prompted a reconsideration of relationships between Christians, Jews, and Muslims and of God's desire that all live together. Somewhat as did ancient Israel, modern Israel, in its struggles to be what its tradition calls it to be, gives rise to renewed reflection about God's way for all humankind. Israel's failures are paralleled in many places around the globe in a variety of conflicts over land. But Israel's standards, based on biblical as well as democratic ideals, are noble and challenge all to a higher way.

In examining the example of modern Israel, a wider, more inclusive vista appears, namely God's desire for all peoples and nations. And what is God's desire? A just peace in which all may live and prosper! A sharing and honoring of God's land, the earth, is God's desire and the challenge placed before each earth keeper. No one can make any of us respond, but all of us know in our hearts that God's way is finally the only way to the security and freedom we all long to enjoy. Shall we join arms and intellects, or shall we continue to twist arms and resist common sense and common cause? Earth keepers, the choice is ours.

QUESTIONS FOR DISCUSSION

1. How do you understand the basic vision and challenge the author presents? How are God, the earth, and human beings interconnected in this vision? Is the vision realistic? What are some of the obstacles?
2. How does the author understand the content and relationship of the terms "peace" and "justice"? How does the Bible help us to understand these terms? Why are they so important?
3. What are the five major issues that must be addressed in working for peace with justice? How can individuals and local groups engage in working for a resolution of these matters? Why is interfaith cooperation so important?
4. What are some of the positive and negative implications of viewing the earth as a sacred trust? Is it legitimate to contend with the author that "A sharing and honoring of God's land, the earth, is God's desire and the challenge placed before each earth keeper"? If so, what is to be done?

FOR FURTHER READING

On Global Land and Ecology Issues

Ambler, Rex. *Global Theology*. Philadelphia: Trinity Press International, 1990.

Evans, Bernard F., and Gregory D. Cusack, eds. *Theology of the Land*. Collegeville, MN: Liturgical Press, 1987.

Granberg-Michaelson, Wesley. *Tending the Garden: Essays on the Gospel and the Earth.* Grand Rapids, MI: Wm. B. Eerdmans, 1987.

Lilburne, Geoffrey R. *A Sense of Place: A Christian Theology of the Land.* Nashville: Abingdon Press, 1989.

May, R. H., Jr. *The Poor of the Land.* Maryknoll, NY: Orbis Books, 1991.

Metz, J. B., and Edward Schillebeeckx, eds. *No Heaven without Earth.* Philadelphia: Trinity Press International, 1991.

Rasmussen, Larry L. *Earth Community, Earth Ethics.* Maryknoll, NY: Orbis Books, 1996.

Restoring Creation for Ecology and Justice. Louisville, KY: Office of the General Assembly, Presbyterian Church (U.S.A.), 1990.

On Justice Issues

Ateek, Naim Stifan. *Justice, and Only Justice: A Palestinian Theology of Liberation.* Maryknoll, NY: Orbis Books, 1989.

Attias, Jean-Christophe, and Esther Benbassa. *Israel, the Impossible Land.* Trans. Susan Emanuel. Stanford, CA: Stanford University Press, 2003.

Friedman, Thomas L. *From Beirut to Jerusalem.* New York: Farrar, Straus & Giroux, 1989.

Ruether, Rosemary Radford, and Herman J. Ruether. *The Wrath of Jonah: The Crisis of Religious Nationalism in the Israeli-Palestinian Conflict.* San Francisco: HarperCollins, 1989.

Stein, Yael. "Land Grab: Israel's Settlement Policy in the West Bank." In *The Struggle for Sovereignty: Palestine and Israel 1993–2005.* Edited by Joel Beinin and Rebecca Stein. Stanford, CA: Stanford University Press, 2006.

Index to Maps